Make It a Habit

365 Daily Inspirational Prompts to Achieve Your Best Self

JACOB SHASHOUA

Producer & International Distributor
eBookPro Publishing
www.ebook-pro.com

MAKE IT A HABIT
Jacob Shashoua
Copyright © 2023 Jacob Shashoua

Contact: kobi.shashoua@gmail.com

ISBN 9798856342122

Contents

Well done!

You are holding this book and not by chance. You're all set. A well-known saying is when the student is ready the teacher arrives.

You're all set, go.

You start a daily journey where you will meet your potential in all areas of your life. You will develop healthy habits and become a better version of yourself.

Do not be afraid to invest, the investment is not much but the secret of development lies in perseverance. The drop is not carved into the rock by the power of its power, but by the power of its perseverance.

It is this perseverance that will open new doors in the depths of your soul, where you will find sources of power and energy waiting to be discovered.

Now is your time!

In this book I have distilled many insights that I have collected over the years from various sources and out of an inner desire to continue to develop and grow spiritually. Much of the knowledge here is intuitive, understandable and even self-explanatory. On each insight you can find endless books and articles written and knowledge is available to everyone.

Knowledge that is laid down as a stone that does not have a reverse does not contribute in any way. Reading in itself is enjoyable, but its contribution is marginal if we do not learn to apply what is written. The practice in practice, the daily training is the one that transforms reality into an area of spiritual growth and development. Bodybuilders have not reached the monstrous proportions from reading material and watching the practices of others. The daily practice, the determination, the belief in the righteousness of the way is what allowed them to fulfill themselves.

Like them, you acted in the same way. Take it to the next step and turn it into a daily plan of action.

Do it with baby steps, slowly but with determination and perseverance. You're going to fall and get up, that's okay. All you have to do is get up just one more time.

When I worked on my dietary habits and made them much healthier, I did so through small changes in my diet. Fruit in the morning is equivalent to an additional 365 fruits per year. Adding some vegetable to each meal adds thousands of vegetables a year. Reducing the amount of sugar in tea from 2 teaspoons to half a teaspoon translates into a reduction of over 500 teaspoons of sugar per year. These small changes have a dramatic impact on health in the long run and do not require a huge investment of energy that ultimately causes most of us to give up and return to Sorino.

I ask you for one thing and that is to spend a few minutes each morning reading the daily page. It is short and sometimes takes less time than brushing your teeth. But it is also important since constant growth and development passes through self-discipline and a daily desire for small changes. Starting the day with a growth insight or positive action will make your day that much more magical. I promise you that reading will become a daily habit and produce miracles in your life. Thinking about insights and taking small positive actions will result in spiritual growth and an increase in happiness levels. Do not give up on yourself because you deserve more. In a short period of time, a tremendous change will take place in you.

I've always loved reading. From a young age, I loved lounging in the school library, reading as many books as possible. I found in the books a source of inexhaustible knowledge. I let my imagination sweep me into different realms and admired the ability of writers to turn an idea into a tangible reality. A genre that I particularly like is the self-help books. In these books I found a rich source of valuable information that allowed me to better understand myself and the world that surrounds me.

The stage where I had to put the book aside and start practicing was the stage where I would usually abandon the book. I was looking for a solution that would not stop my personal and spiritual growth. I was looking for an easy solution to implement.

Leo Tolstoy's 1906 book The Reading Class was an inspiration for me. The book consists of daily pages, the reading of which is done according to the date of that day. I enjoyed reading the book daily usually in the morning. I found that the book is up-to-date and concentrates on sayings, insights and theological and religious proverbs appropriate to the period in which it was published. I was missing something up-to-date that fits the modern lifestyle, that I could connect to on an immediate level, that would speak to me at eye level and allow me to experience the current reality. It was then that I had a burning desire to write an up-to-date, contemporary book, easy to apply to understand and connect.

Thus, over the years, I found myself recording insights on top of insights from my daily life. Slowly the notebook filled up. These insights have become this book that you hold in your hands. A book that will make a huge difference in you.

These insights were written over the course of several years and after personal experience and a process of spiritual growth that

I have been experiencing for over a decade. When I look back, I am amazed at the way and the change that has occurred in me over the years. I guess my previous career pushed me to look for inner meaning. During the 20 years of working as a broker, I felt a growing lack of meaning and purpose. The constant preoccupation with investments with random results, the incessant pursuit of the next good investment. The total lack of control over what could happen and the intense preoccupation with this world have opened a growing abyss within me. I found myself slowly drawn to the spiritual realm looking for meaning and a desire to create real value that would touch as many people as possible. Thus was born the idea of writing a simple daily guide that is accessible to everyone and from personal experience I submit this guide. Reading it daily will create over time tremendous spiritual growth in each and every one. In the end if I had to summarize spiritual growth in a few words then I would say that spiritual growth means the silent acceptance of things as they are. This is not a trivial sentence. We experience objections, frustrations, upsets, accusations, grumble and angry and in the end if we really learn to accept the here and now as it is then we will not need these emotions and thoughts to navigate our world. If we detail spiritual growth, then I am talking about achieving peace within me in all my parts. Adopting authentic peace and relaxation as a way of life. Slowing down the pace and enhancing our presence in everything. To this package I would add the abolition of judgment, and criticality or our tendency to desire and replace this with a deep demand to live life in a light-hearted manner.

The insights do not concentrate solely on the spiritual world, other insights are from the field of finance, nutrition, sports, fitness family, friends, etc.

The insights are practical and easy to implement. The investment is minor and amounts to a few minutes of reading and digestion. The insights will resonate in your mind throughout the day and daily reading will change your mind in an imperceptible but powerful way. The insights are not burdensome and overall intuitive and easy to understand and agree with. I am confident that you will benefit greatly from this number and achieve new levels of calm and calm and the accompanying reward is a continuous increase in happiness levels.

How to use this book

There's nothing like the quiet of the morning to make a huge difference in your daily routine. This quietness is available for everyone. Even if your morning routine is an endless race to get everything ready and run to work, it's because of the habits you've adopted.

For years I have had the habit of waking up before everyone else so I can sit quietly by myself, meditate and read.

For me, reading is used as a tool for spiritual growth and development.

My days now look different than before. Reading a page of this book each morning will help you start the day with anticipation and optimism. There is something magical about the early, silent hours of the morning. we are able to soak up the most information in the morning.

There is no better time to practice positivity and optimism, and start the day with a smile.

The wisdom in this book is easy to understand.

Although I often speak about practical and actionable wisdom the focus on how to do it is less relevant; for every piece of wisdom, even the smallest one, there is a wealth of information and books on it.

A good example that illustrates the essential difference between the "why" and the "how" is through the saying, "Those who know how to do things will always work under those who know why." The "why" is the key, the awareness, the invested thought, the attempt to develop and grow. In this book I have placed an emphasis on the "why" – which is the heart of this book – to awaken awareness, thought, desire and desire – once they exist the "how" will be simple to implement.

As you read, you will notice that sometimes I will summarize daily insight with active action and sometimes I will simply ask you to present it in your life.

Some of the insights will resonate with you and you will feel a powerful connection to them and some will not even relate or that will seem irrelevant to you. It is ok. As part of a broad human fabric we are different and diverse but we will never stop learning and developing if we want to and also from the things that seem clear to us there is a lot to learn.

So the best time to start is now!

Open the book on the page with the relevant date and start a magical journey for the rest of your life!

January

January 1ˢᵗ

A New Year has begun.

New hopes, old dreams, new dreams...

A new year is an opportunity to forget the old and bring in the new.

It doesn't matter if you succeeded at everything and achieved what you wanted. This is a new opportunity to reinvent yourself. The truth is that the end result is less important than you think. It doesn't matter if you've achieved everything you've promised yourself, the important thing is that you create awareness of what's important to you and what will create a valuable and fulfilling life for you. Your awareness and mental tuning will work to get you there. Most likely the road is longer than expected and most of our goals aren't going to be realized within a defined period of time. What's most important is the point at the beginning of the year when there's the greatest cosmic awareness regarding what's most important to you. Write it down and integrate it into your consciousness. Act each day, one step at a time towards your goal. Remember that the result is not as important as the path. Use gentle refining to figure out what is best for you.

Happy New Year!

January 2nd

Don't let a few tough minutes ruin your day.
It happens sometimes. Someone cuts you off in traffic or cuts you in line. Someone does an injustice against you. You could choose to get upset or you could choose not to, but even though you choose not to, your body may decide differently and your heart will beat rapidly. This experience is the "fight or flight" response that psychologists have studied for centuries. The goal then, is to shorten the amount of time we feel fear and anxiety. Some of us walk around feeling panicked for days as though something life-changing had occurred. Many also walk around sad or angry, but quickly perk up to discuss their agonies with anyone that will listen. But ultimately, we have the responsibility to minimize the amount of time we feel negatively. Don't let these few minutes ruin an entire day.

So what can you do if you've had an unpleasant experience? Allow yourself to be fully immersed in the experience for a while. Be mindful that it is up to you to reduce the suffering and frustration your misplaced anxiety has caused. Once you are able to take control of your thoughts you will be rewarded with peace.

How do we attain peace? Start with knowing that your mind can only hold one thought at a time and then take control of your thought process. Decide to look at the situation with humor or simply repeat the mantra "I love myself". You can also think of a positive event that is coming up or look up into the night sky and understand how insignificant we all are compared to the universe. We are a miracle and we should focus on living life instead of focusing on the setbacks.

January 3rd

The illusion that you are in control.

We all want control, but the only thing we can control is our conscious choices. Control isn't real, it's an illusion and it's always accompanied with a heavy price. We can make plans, but in the blink of an eye, everything will change. These kinds of situations may destroy people who have an immense need for control. Research has found that the need to control is structured from childhood. We want to control everything we can so that the element of surprise is pushed to the curb. A strong need to control can permeate all the levels of our lives and affect people with whom we interact. We try to control our parents, other family members, friends, colleagues, etc. We want to control our destiny and our future, but it's impossible. It's an illusion. This illusion turns those who are addicted to control into irritable, anxious, stressed and tense people. We must internalize that we have no control over anything, only over our conscious choices. Many spend their energy on controlling the events in their life and often suffer defeat.

So, what is the solution? A new and fresh way of thinking. There's nothing like peace of mind in acceptance, surrendering to the present, and the freedom to choose our thoughts, feelings and behaviors at any given time. All of this will treat our souls and prepare us to successfully deal with unforeseen events. We can act effectively and not waste our energy on trying to control the circumstances. We may be walking on the right path, but the future is still a mystery. That's okay, this is life, accept it humbly.

Today, adopt the mindset that accepts lovingly what there is and what will be. Everything is fine!

January 4th

Look life directly in the eyes. There's nothing to be afraid of.

We are blessed in the modern age. This time holds endless opportunities for fascinating and exciting discoveries. Thanks to technology, life is much easier and simpler than it used to be. What used to be science *fiction* is now our daily reality. There's no doubt we're living in one of the most fascinating periods in human history. The information revolution and its availability create infinite possibilities for exploration and improvement. But technology is also a thorn, it has negative sides.

Social networking, instant messaging, virtual reality, Facebook, Instagram, etc, avoids the fact that we should spend more time with real people in real life. Through social media platforms we have the ability to gather thousands of people we've never met before into a virtual space. We call these people friends which shows that the definition of the word friend is changing compared to how our parents and grandparents used it. A continuous lack of human interaction will cause us to lose our ability to develop social relationships, and may even turn us into emotionless non-empathetic robots. This inability harms us as human beings as we need social interaction. The disappearance of social relationships can cause loneliness, depression, low self-worth and self-esteem. Social interaction is a basic need so we must cultivate it for our daily life. Dare to look into someone's eyes when connecting socially. Shake their hand and deliver a message of existence, humanity and joy.

Today, really see the people you come in contact with! Be interested in their well-being! Ask questions, listen to their answers... and smile! You aren't a robot, you're a human being. Act like it!

January 5th

Choose the type of fuel you want to consume.

There's a relationship between our body and soul that I assume most people are aware of. It's a connection that develops the moment we come into the world. There are fields in modern medicine which tend to neglect the existence of the soul and focus mainly on the physiological side. This disbelief manifests itself in the treatment of symptoms without holistic vision. Sometimes it seems that getting sick, tired or ill-tempered is due to a weak immune system when it actually stems from an injured or battered soul.

Our bodies should be filled with fuel that allows it to operate at its best. We also require fuel specifically suited to us as individuals so that we can function at our best.

So what do I mean by fuel?

By choosing to entertain only positive thoughts such as compassion, self-love, self-acceptance, and joy, any negative thoughts will be quickly neutralized.

Setting some basic rules would significantly improve the type of fuel we use to drive our body and soul. By reducing the amount of sugar, simple carbohydrates and dairy products we could drastically improve our well-being. We should chew our food slowly and make sure it's high in calories, complex carbohydrates, quality protein, and healthy fats (which you can get from nuts- they are full of it). Eat fruits, vegetables and drink water, lots of water, to become a healthier and happier you.

Start now! Replace every harmful ingredient with a healthier one, then meditate on the change you made for a short time. The main thing is that you get started, slowly, choosing what is best for you until it becomes a habit.

I urge you to do this, the benefits are incredible!

January 6th

Before change shows externally we must change within.

Part of being human means we carry a sophisticated machine that constantly complains. It's okay, don't whine about it. Without even noticing spit out a shower of complaints. We try to change our world so that it will fit into the ideas we've developed about it. No wonder we find ourselves unhappy. We try to change the behavior of those around us. However, the environment and people around us are a reflection of us. We are in a bubble that is constructed of the decisions and choices we've made in our lives. Some things are fixed like family and friends. When we try to change the unchangeable our attempts often end in unnecessary frustration and anger. The question we need to answer is do our surroundings have to change or does the change need to come from within? Control is an illusion, that's why trying to get it often ends in failure and disappointment.

The correct way is to realize that real change comes internally. Change yourself and your perception and reality will follow. To accomplish this you must take responsibility for yourself, your thoughts and your feelings. Change what's not working for you, do it step by step, day after day, with perseverance and determination. Eventually, change will seep out from you.

Today, accept your complaints with compassion. Listen to them calmly, but don't let it affect your soul. Act tirelessly to create change slowly, day by day, with determination and perseverance. The change in you will reflect your reality and will even affect those around you.

January 7th

Is it time to take a risk?

Life passes as we follow our path. A lot of the time we are on autopilot. Waking up in the morning and getting ready is done almost automatically. The morning coffee, taking the same lane at the same time and driving the same congested road have become the norm. Work has also become automatic. Many times our lives can seem banal. We only feel excitement when we complain about our general dissatisfaction, the high taxes, low wages, the country we live in, neighbors, spouses, children and jobs. There's no doubt that the repetitive nature of routine is what wears us down, as anything done over and over again does.

Life's journey can be boring and predictable, ending with a tombstone that reads: "He who lies here... was not very interesting." Your life can be a boring walk or an interesting roller coaster ride, but it's your roller coaster and you must ride it. If you treat everything as an adventure then life will be more interesting. Why not "take a chance" on something that will put some spice into your routine? Why not dare? The worst thing that could happen is that *nothing* will happen! The best thing is that you tried and most likely succeeded!

Today, do something daring. Do it because you deserve it!

January 8th

It's all bullshit.
Life is short and days pass by like leaves in the wind. One day we'll *all* be stardust again; it'll happen for sure so in the meantime all there is left to do is live. Our lives expand and shrink according to the degree of courage we have. Dare to make brave decisions that will take you to wonderful places. Remember that we're all eventually washed downstream and the only way to utilize our days is to live them to the fullest. It's hard on a daily basis, but try to do a small brave act today, something unusual, something that will put a smile on your face. Count this as another small victory.

I'd like to illustrate the meaning of my life in the following short story.

A great-grandmother was dying and the entire family had gathered around her. She'd lived a meaningful life filled with infatuations, disappointments, two marriages, three children, eight grandchildren, and she'd even lived to experience four great-grandchildren.

On her deathbed, with all the strength left in her, she requested to speak with her eldest daughter. She asked her daughter to bend down and she whispered a few words in her ear, and then she breathed her last breath.

The family members, though shocked, asked to know what the grandmother's last words were.

The eldest daughter turned to them and said, "She told me it's all bullshit!"

January 9th

It's time to give up control. Oh, how we long for it. We think and feel that we have control over the people in our lives and our surroundings, but it's an illusion. We believe that we have the ability to control events and direct them in our favor. Maybe we can sometimes, but it's only partial in the end. How many times have we experienced situations where it got out of hand? Those around us turn out to have their own opinions. This is doubly true with our immediate family. Our partners make their own decisions, and let's not talk about the children who do whatever they want. One must internalize and understand that control is an illusion and the appropriate word to replace it with is Responsibility. Instead of trying to control things and being disappointed time after time, we must take responsibility and control what we can: our reaction. A famous concept about control is that it's made of two parts; 10% is our control over events and situations and 90% is our reaction. If we continue to try to control life's events we'll be disappointed. However, if we understand that we have limited control over situations in our lives we can then take responsibility for our reactions. Then, we have control. We are the only ones responsible for our reactions.

Think about it today and try to adopt this concept. It will allow you to regain control of your reactions to events, people and circumstances.

January 10th

The greatest sin we inflict upon ourselves is _____ _____ for granted. Life is a miracle and time is shorter than we think.

We must not forget this intuitive understanding that will allow us to forgive others, forgive ourselves and cherish the miracle of life.

In Judaism it's custom to say this morning prayer when waking up: "I thank you living and enduring King, for you have graciously returned my soul to me this day. Great is your faithfulness." The power of this prayer is the prayer itself. It's power stems from the soul's recognition of its nothingness in the face of the Majesty.

Your thoughts and feelings in the morning will largely determine the rest of your day. Start the day with a prayer and you are guaranteed to feel better for the rest of the day.

It has nothing to do with the degree of your religion or your ethnic background. Reciting this prayer every morning will improve how you feel. Praying will allow you to start the day differently. It takes 12 seconds to recite this prayer. Stop making excuses! If you make a promise to yourself to wake up like this every morning, I guarantee that your happiness will skyrocket.

January 11th

Smile often!

The value of a smile is priceless. A smile is a tool we can learn to use all the time. It melts stress, is easy to use and the results are immediate. It affects the external world just like it affects the internal. Smiles are contagious. It will relieve your stress, create new energy and stimulate your soul!

Smile now!

January 12th

Stop!

Autopilot controls us and routine is king, but do we really want to live like that? Is that the kind of life we want for ourselves? The answer is most likely No for most of us! You can let fate decide what does and doesn't go on sale, but not what does and doesn't happen in your life! Consumerism has imprisoned us in a giant rat race. Fast food and the internet are just symptoms of the bigger problems. There is a call for more, more and more... Bigger houses, more cars, better iPhones. Like drug addicts we flock to the new trends, trying to give the last of our dollar to own the most fashionable widget.

We're responsible for stopping the rat race because we created it. Every day we face a choice; should we continue on as we are or find another way to live our lives? Is this what we really want? Wouldn't you be willing to consider serenity? Ask yourself one simple question, is this the best way for me to live my life?

Think about it today. This is a question you must ask yourself from time to time. Consider it the key to "keeping it real".

January 13th

"See, I set before you today life and prosperity, death and destruction... then you will live and increase."
Deuteronomy 30:15

It's obvious that we've chosen life since we're alive. But did we really choose? Some of us woke up this morning for only one reason, we didn't die overnight. Life *must* be chosen consciously because if it's not we just simply exist. Life passes without fulfillment when we act randomly, without goals or consciously choosing a path.

We must be responsible for our lives, otherwise randomness will run it. You're the captain of your life. Life is the ship sailing in the sea. If you don't navigate it, it will sail aimlessly reaching different destinations than you've intended or worse, run aground. You must consciously choose life! You must consciously choose good! You're responsible and you're the navigator.

Today, write who you are with sincerity. Write about where you want to be in life and build yourself an organized plan full of actions you can take. Make them step by step. Greg Reid said, "A dream written down with a date becomes a goal. A goal broken down into steps becomes a plan. A plan that is backed by action makes your dreams come true."

January 14th

What makes us feel better?

We've all had one of those days. It's normal and it's part of being human. What can we do about it? We have the option to whine or, if we put a bit of effort, we can improve our situation. We must remember that a change in attitude can change our negative energy. I know it's not always easy, but the alternative is worse. In everything and every situation there's always something positive.

Stop for a moment, look up at the sky and stop and smell the roses. If you're lucky you'll see birds flying above. Bless yourself for who you are and what you are, the miracle of creation! Life was given as a gift to the lucky ones and you're one of them.

There will always be things that won't work and circumstances that are not in your favor. That's how it was and that's how it will be. What matters is your approach to it all. Don't give up on yourself. Remember that you deserve to feel good!

January 15th

I'm sure it's happened to you; you've felt inferior to someone else. The feeling of inferiority gnaws at your self-image and self-confidence and makes you doubt yourself and your abilities. This can eventually lead to poor performance or even paralysis.

I ask that you never allow yourself to feel inferior again!

Look at our leaders. How did they succeed? The world is in financial crisis, there are endless wars, refugee crises, epidemics, a pandemic and climate change. It seems that those "geniuses" fail time and time again, but it doesn't gnaw at their confidence. They are still sure they will succeed no matter what. Why do they feel that way when you don't? Why don't you feel as valuable? You aren't inferior to them. At the end of the day they don't know any more than you. They just believe in themselves and they don't let others' judgments affect them.

Hone those abilities. It's a conscious choice. You aren't inferior, you're a human being. You're allowed to succeed. You're allowed to make mistakes and despite everything, you're also allowed to walk forward when you're finished screwing up.

January 16th

The power of words.

Words can create and also destroy. Those who despise the power of words, words despise them back. It's not by chance that ancient wisdom preached, "life and death is in the power of the tongue." Words have the power to create reality. There's a constant monologue in our minds and we are silent guests. Our thoughts are constant and the words used impact us immensely. Our own beliefs about ourselves are much stronger than those said by others.

Many people underestimate themselves and use words that diminish their worth. They say things like, "I'm such an idiot." "This is going to be a nightmare." "I can't believe this is happening to me again." If you've already decided you're an idiot, who am I to argue with you, even if you said it as a joke. This is where the problem lies, in the negative, yet unconscious perception of ourselves and presentation of ourselves to others. We must be aware of the destructive power of words.

You aren't stupid, you're human and its fact that we make mistakes. The only ones who are never wrong are those who offer nothing. If you've decided that something is going to be a nightmare, then it's going to be a nightmare because that's what you've manifested. Do you understand the power of words? We need to use them in our favor.

From now on practice using positive language by using words like compassion, acceptance, love, peace and serenity. Create kindness inside yourself and pay attention to the words you're using with yourself and others. It's another challenge and only good will come out of it.

January 17th

In hindsight things feel less scary than they once were.
The roadblocks and hurdles we overcome seem miniscule when we look back on them. Sometimes, fear prevents us from doing the thing that is right for us.

Life is growth, and growth is change. It's hard to incorporate this philosophy into our lives so we sometimes find ourselves stuck in our comfort zones. The fear of change sometimes prevents us from doing the right thing. Fear has its allies like excuses, doubt and reasons why change is a threat.

Stop for a moment and think of all the changes you've experienced in your life, whether it was a painful breakup, a career change, or moving. No doubt before every major event there was fear surrounding you, but in hindsight you probably know that it wasn't as bad as you'd imagined.

Remember that most people don't regret the things that they did, but the things that they didn't do! Avoid regrets at all costs because the price is high. Every time you're about to make a positive change but get scared, imagine that you're in the future and look back on the decision. How ridiculous is your fear!

January 18th

Our physical discomfort is often due to our mental state.

I will risk saying that the vast majority of cases of physical exhaustion stem from emotional exhaustion. Western medicine has a tendency to focus on the physical body and ignore the body-mind connection. Fatigue is attributed to the problems in our liver, kidneys, lungs, etc. Blood tests and other medical examinations attempt to figure out the physical problem and solve it with prescribed medication. Let's stop for a moment. Maybe the problem is mental and a pill's not going to help it!

Repressed fear, unfulfilled desires and hidden resentments cause internal conflict. Conflict is a waste of energy and something no medical device or test can detect. So, what's the solution? It's not easy, but it's a must. Simply, be honest with yourself, acknowledge your weak spots and accept your only human and you're doing the best you can.

If you're exhausted it's time to investigate what's *not* working and find out what's stopping you from attaining your true desires. Bravely look at your weak spots and release the energy that is trapped within you.

You'll feel refreshed and at peace the moment you stop resisting change.

January 19th

Life isn't fair.

Sometimes we find ourselves at rock bottom and at other times on the top of the world. Throughout both we have our ability to make decisions about our lives in the areas that we can. That's a lot of power!

Sometimes we find ourselves in unjust situations that are out of our hands so we must stand up for ourselves and clarify our point of view without fear because no one else will. This grand process is accompanied by fear. That fear is legitimate and exists to protect us.

Even if you were wronged, be aware of your thoughts, feelings and actions and make them work for you. It's not always easy, but it's the right thing to do.

January 20ᵗʰ

It's necessary to set goals.

It allows us to follow a guideline and move closer to what we want. Keep in mind that a goal isn't a vision of our future, it just brings us along a certain path that we must travel. The path is our life and we have to enjoy it as we walk it. We must do everything we can to enjoy the journey and learn from it. Our goal is not the finish line.

The path is sometimes long and winding. For example, obtaining a diploma takes years of lessons, exams and learning. Graduation is only an hour long, but it takes those years of hard work to reach that moment. And look at those who reached the top of Mt. Everest. It took years of mental preparation, physical training, trial runs and climbing sessions to make it happen. The actual time spent at the summit was minimal when compared to the time spent preparing. Reaching the top is not what determines their worthiness, but it's their whole journey from start to finish that's their greatest success.

Today, choose a goal that is challenging for you. Enjoy the path and know that the objective is not to finish, but to enjoy what happens along the way.

January 21th

A bit about pain.
The fear of failure can sometimes prevent someone from taking action. But, if we don't try, we don't experience risk or pain. (We've already talked about avoidance and its futility.) When we experience change or pain we can grow to become someone we admire.

We usually treat the pain of failure as an enemy, but we should embrace it with gratitude. Bodybuilders reach their goals through tough, painful exercise. Marathon runners improve their abilities by consistently pushing their pain threshold. Birth reminds us that determination rewards us when we hold our child in our arms. Turn pain into your friend. Bring it into your heart and learn its lessons. Remember that pain builds resilience, without pain you can't know joy. Repeat the phrase, "No pain, no gain" as you struggle.

Failure is accompanied by pain, but it's required for our growth. You're only human. Forgive yourself your shortcomings.

January 22th

If you can't compliment yourself, at least be kind.

If you find yourself thinking negatively about or saying unkind words to yourself, you're in a troublesome place. It's easy to get carried away and say how terrible we are. We try to get pity or support while promising ourselves that it's the last time that we'll try something difficult because we didn't get the outcome we wanted or we were disappointed. Words have the power to build bridges or build walls.

Words that are casually said are the most telling. There's an important audience of listeners every time we open our mouths. First, we are listening to *ourselves* and unconsciously act on our words. Second, the Universe is listening and working on what we asked for. If what we ask for is negative, limiting, or inhibiting, the Universe will provide. The saying, "Be careful what you wish for" is undoubtedly true.

Why speak ill of yourself? We're only human. We're not perfect. We'll continue to make mistakes and fail. We'll be disappointed over and over again. Sometimes we'll feel helpless and small and sometimes we'll feel elevated and grateful. That's life. Everything is okay and normal and perfectly fine. Let's continue to appreciate our past mistakes and the lessons they taught us. Let's forgive ourselves! No one is perfect!

January 23th

What's around us is not always real.

Whether it's a fake smile, an automatic greeting, good morning wishes, your boss feigning toughness or you pretending to be someone you are not, these gestures secretly manifest themselves in strenuous ways.

Our society glorifies strength, rigidity and efficiency. Movies are full of fearless heroes, but life on screen is completely different from what most of us face each morning. What would happen if you stopped faking and simply surrendered? Show your humanity for better or worse and don't worry about winning the race today. Do you think that endlessly pretending doesn't involve tension so that your "scam" won't be discovered? Don't you see that you're only as tough as you're pretending to be? What would happen if the covers were pulled back and the truth was exposed? Would you be a different person than you are right now?

Pay attention to who you are attracted to. Are the people that turn your head creating a false image or are they being themselves? Are they fake or are they living without calculating what others will think before they do something? Do they live without needing to impress anyone? Do you surround yourself with the real or the make-believe? What would happen if for one day we all stopped faking it and simply presented ourselves to the world?

Try this today. The humanity within you will be rewarded with growth, far more than the fake persona you may have developed.

January 24ᵗʰ

Setting a goal is not always an easy task.

Sometimes we set the bar a little too low and make our goals too easy. There's nothing wrong with taking it easy as long as it doesn't become a habit. However, if we don't believe we can achieve our goals (aka setting them too high), we will then deem them impossible and give up. The best way to reach our full potential is to set goals that are challenging, but still achievable.

It's similar to driving a car with a GPS. We first choose our destination and then the GPS navigates there one street at a time. If we believe our goal is achievable, then we will be able to take steps forward. After that, the hardest thing to do is persevere. Focus your efforts and don't digress. Your steps will lead you to your goal.

Remember the saying of Chinese philosopher Laozi, "A journey of a thousand miles begins with a single step." *(Dao De Jing Chapter 6-4)*

January 25th

The process of spiritual growth, or any growth, contains struggle.

Struggle doesn't always mean pain, but a "passage through resistance". Chicks that hatch from eggs can't instantly fly. Their ability to fly develops after countless attempts and countless amounts of practice. If you want to fly you must try your wings long before you leave the safety of the ground. Life is full of trials and challenges and going through them and changing because of them is what makes you unique.

Taking on challenges is what makes your life meaningful and what makes your life different from someone else's. So, what challenge will you meet today?

January 26th

A question for your soul: Whose life is this?

Is it truly yours? If you're claiming yes, then act like it is yours. What kind of life do you have? Do the choices you make come from your heart or are they dictated by your environment? Are you living to fulfill your own expectations or someone else's? Are you fulfilled by the path you're taking or are you regretful? Have you chosen this path or were you forced to take it?

Near the end of your life you'll ask, did I live for myself? Was I happy?

Today, think your own thoughts and practice awareness.

January 27th

Reflections for a new day.

Why did you get up this morning? Was it an automatic, unconscious action?

The universe is infinite and in comparison we are as small as dust. So, why does it matter how we live our lives when our time is short and inconsequential? What prevents us from reaching our potential? We all have an inner compass. Let's listen to it and see where it leads us. Life is a journey that can be fascinating and amazing, but it's up to you. Walking a path that has been taken many times before will lead you to where others have gone. Be original- take the fork. Don't be part of the machine.

What matters is what you want to be, not who, but *what*! Today, think about what your values are and what steps you take to live them out.

Good morning and have a lovely day.

January 28th

Look for the hidden motive.

Everything has a reason. It's not always obvious. If you want to better understand yourself, others, and the universe then look for the hidden motives. By understanding the hidden motive you will be able to understand the process behind what motivates you and others. For example, does your boss push you to finish a project on time because it reflects well on you? Or is it because they are guaranteed a fat bonus if the deadline is met? Being able to understand a boss's motives will benefit you; you'll be able to decide the best way to proceed and how to make things work in your favor. You would be able to cooperate with him more fully and obtain his appreciation... perhaps even a bonus yourself.

Does a student's desire to study with another student that they find attractive stem from mutual inspiration and exchange of knowledge? Or do they think that it would be an opportunity to create something romantic? By understanding hidden motives it will allow you to achieve better, more fruitful and helpful relationships.

Think about your actions today and watch those around you. What are the hidden motives and how can you use what you see to your advantage?

January 29th

Who pulls the strings? Is it you? Your friends, family, manager, partner?

We often wonder how we got here. Were our actions and choices really ours? Were they conscious? Were they performed to serve us? And if not, then who?

If you find yourself somewhere other than where you want to be, if you've behaved wrongly or made bad choices, then stop and think about what brought you here. Stop the chatter in your mind, replan your path and think about what inspires you.

Pull your own strings. Create your plan because if you don't someone else will. Sail your own ship.

January 30th

The measuring gauges in the car reflect its "mood".

The higher the number the more stressed the vehicle is. The car could be moving uphill or trying to accelerate. Too much stress could result in expedited wear and tear (and burning unnecessary fuel). Most often we keep our gauges at normal levels. After exerting much effort we must let up on the gas and allow our gauges to return to normal. The ride then becomes relaxed and routine.

However, anger, rage, or tension raises the number on our gauges. We're alert, with adrenaline flowing through us and we're ready to fight. But, like a car, we aren't able to maintain this heightened state for long before exhaustion hits. Since we don't actually have a way to measure our "gauges" we tend to stay in our heightened states for long periods of time and wear our bodies and minds out. The wear and tear eventually appears in the form of mental illness or physical disease. We must remember that being on 100% is intended for short periods of time and that our natural state is slow, calm and peaceful. No matter what the circumstances are, we must learn to take care of ourselves and keep our gauge numbers low.

What are your normal gauge numbers? What are they now?

January 31th

The law of large numbers.

The law of large numbers says that if we repeat an action multiple times we have better chances at getting our desired result. The best example of this is when we talk about sales. Salespeople start with a large number of potential customers knowing that most of them will refuse their deal. Eventually some of the potential clients will be interested, and then a smaller number will actually purchase the product.

If we want to succeed in a project or goal then we must understand and harness the power of the law of large numbers. Sometimes we start a new project, whether professional or personal, and after countless attempts without the desired result we despair and contemplate giving up. It's okay to fail and keep going. The law of large numbers determines that after a certain amount of "no's" we'll most likely get a "yes".

I'm guessing you've heard of the movie Rocky. The star of the movie, Sylvester Stallone, wrote the script. Many studios rejected it, but he didn't let "no" stop him. He knew that the day would come that he would hear a "yes". The rest is history.

And you! How many times have you heard "no" and given up? Sometimes it takes a few more "no's" to get to that "yes". Don't let a "no" make you give up your goal!

February

February 1st

It isn't personal.
Sometimes it seems like everything is against us, like dark forces have joined hands in order to defeat us, but after a while the storm subsides and calmness returns. What caused the storm in the first place? One cause could be our never-ending thoughts. Negative thoughts are like a disease. This disease creates our perception of reality, which in turn causes more negative thoughts. Over time these thoughts slowly weaken and the negative cycle breaks. Just like that of a storm, we also return to normal.

What can we do? It's important to be aware of our thoughts and when they unconsciously become negative. This is important because we can then cut down the trees of negative thoughts and plant seeds of hope and new beliefs. Once you act with awareness and replace negative thoughts with positive ones you will get great results.

Today, be aware of your thoughts and replace negative thoughts with positive ones. Being conscious of what is happening inside your mind will guarantee you peace of mind.

February 2nd

Are you free?

Many dreams about the moment when they'll be free and happy. When will this moment arrive? When we are rich enough? Retired? When our children leave the house? These moments have a tendency of not arriving. It has nothing to do with our circumstances, we just don't allow ourselves to make the inner choice to be free. Even the richest people have feelings that their money might run out one day or disappear, and so they become enslaved to their own wealth. They never allow themselves to enjoy their own money.

What is wealth then? It's a person who has everything. It could be a bum dozing on the bench! The real freedom is spiritual, it's freedom to feel whole or to feel like a part of the miracle of life or freedom to understand yourself and everything else. You'll never be able to satisfy everybody 100%, there are always going to be those who won't appreciate you. There will be those who try to tease you, some will even humiliate, despise and control you. Real freedom, then, is achieved when you distinguish yourself from everyone else and decide to become your own person. Freedom is achieved when you realize that you are not inferior to anyone and don't try to change others' thoughts since you have no control over them. Know who you are and be satisfied with that because some will never know. You'll never be liked by everyone so don't try, (unless you want to be the president). Neither your freedom nor your happiness depends on other people. Don't give others the power to control your thoughts.

February 3rd

Learn to trust yourself.

This title doesn't refer to the big things in life, but the banal things like the daily routine. We live in an era where there are experts for everything. We have been taught to be skeptical about our personal choices and therefore we're told that we need to consult with experts for the best answers. Listening to the advice of others isn't a bad thing in itself. The problems start when you become dependent on your experts and can no longer make choices for yourself. By saying "learn to trust yourself" I mean that you already have the tools you need to make the right choice. Listen to your inner voice that is whispering to you, it knows what's best for you. When you consult other people you get their advice according to their point of view, personal experience, failures or successes. No one has a monopoly on knowledge. People who are seriously ill consult with many experts and receive a range of opinions and possibilities before taking action. There is no one opinion that is right and the one who has to decide ultimately is you. It's true that it's convenient to let others decide for you but the price that comes with it could be high.

When Bill Gates was asked what would have happened if he had listened to his parents advice he said that he would have most likely become a university professor. Listen to others, but make your own choice! You know what's best for you. Learn to listen and trust your instincts and your intuition, it's always on your side!

Today, practice being silent and listen to the whispers that go through your mind. What are they trying to tell you? If you're undecided, stop for a moment and listen to your inner voice, the answer is always there.

February 4th

Allow yourself to be silly.

Kids are silly all day. However, if adults did the same it would be perceived as irresponsible and could even provoke contempt.

Adults can sometimes be silly even if they aren't aware of it. There's no doubt that alcohol can make people act silly. Although the silly behavior is not normal it's forgivable because it was caused by intoxication.

This spirit of mischief exists in every one of us and we don't have to finish a few bottles of alcohol to bring it out. Being silly is a tool that successful comedians use. We rush to the cinema and pay money to see actors being silly in comedies. We're also silly with ourselves in our own company.

Allow yourself to unwind. Be silly as much as you please, you don't need a drink to feel like a kid. If you're on your own, no one will see and no one will tell.

February 5ᵗʰ

How did I get here? Are things in my life a coincidence or decided by fate? Is this all there is? Do I have any part in what is happening to me? Where do I fit in?!

The answers to life's questions are complicated for everyone. Where you were born and the family you grew up with influence your life, unlike the man standing next to you who had a completely different experience. Our starting points are not the same and some have better beginnings than others, however, the difference in your upbringing is not a reason to give up on infinite abundance or settle for too little.

Our journey becomes our responsibility from the moment we start to think independently. It's not always easy to change your circumstances and things don't always make sense, but that's life. I'm just laying out the rules of the game. Ultimately, what happens each day and what you find yourself living in is a result of how well you're managing your thoughts. Remember Anais Nin's saying, "Life shrinks or expands in proportion to one's courage." Be brave and get out of your comfort zone. The road you travel might be bumpy at times, but remember it's your road. Be proud of yourself, you can only walk your path once so make sure it's worth it.

Want to know what's going on inside your head? Pay attention to your surroundings, it's the direct result of your thoughts. Your thoughts turn into beliefs, then into feelings and actions. To get different results you can change your thoughts, which will manifest into different actions. It depends on you and only you.

Do it now! Change your thoughts, dare, try, try, fail, and try again. It's okay to fail, it's your job as the leader of your future!

February 6th

Who doesn't like receiving compliments?

A compliment is a positive affirmation that we are loved and wanted, but it is not all that it seems.

Addiction to compliments causes our emotions to be controlled by what others say. As children we long to be seen, appreciated, cherished and loved. As adults these longings haven't passed and sometimes it runs our lives when it shouldn't be.

We have no control over the thoughts of others. If your supervisor doesn't appreciate you, that's okay. Maybe you could try changing his opinion about you, but you shouldn't let his opinion affect everything. We can't allow others to control us or determine what we believe about ourselves. Unfortunately, we fall into this trap often. Whether consciously or unconsciously we do things or behave in certain ways to elicit the compliments we need from others, and when we can't do it then woe is us. Giving others the key to our emotions is an awful way to live. It doesn't have to be this way.

You must remember that you're valuable just by being human and not because of what someone says to you. You're valuable, not because of the amount in your bank account or the success or awards you've received in your life, you're valuable because you've decided you are! That's the only reason you need!

So decide right now that you are valuable!

February 7th

>0

(Greater than zero).

Many times we're attacked by fear. Doubts fill us and prevent us from doing the right thing, even if it only requires a small amount of courage. Feelings of regret are overwhelming when we see other people achieve what we don't think we can.

Think about your problem numerically, see that the thing that we want as greater than zero. Neutralize your emotions regardless of the results you want. Overcome the fear, shame and doubts, and gather the necessary courage to go and get what you want. Focus on the target and conquer it. The worst-case scenario is that you don't succeed. The result when you fail is no change at all and will equal zero. However, by achieving your goal (or even a small part of it), you will always be left with more than what you had before... >0.

Conclusion: Your situation will always improve when you try. At best you succeed and at worst nothing happens. The most important thing is that you tried!

Today, find a challenge. Maybe it's something you've wanted to do for a long time, but had all the "right" reasons for not doing it. At best you might succeed!

February 8th

Do not let who you are interfere with who you can be.
In life there will be times where we will regret that we aren't like our heroes. If we had the fortitude of a superhero we could get over any difficulty or obstacle in our life. Often our heroes are actually actors who lack the traits and abilities of their character. However, the actors are not put down by this obstacle. Often, even bad actors take on the challenge of playing characters who are far different from them.

Who could you play? Maybe you could play your own hero for a change! Imagine what you could do if you let go of the chain that binds you, whether its links are made of self-doubt, fear or lack of initiative. What could you achieve then, you and no one else?

You may discover that you sabotage your own success. You don't do it purposely. Usually, it's fear that serves as a defense mechanism against any change that comes with risk. In modern life the risk isn't tangible or physical if it's fear of failure or rejection. Be aware of that, don't stay in one place. Try and fail, but never fail to try. Walk around with that insight and be aware of what is driving you. Where in your life do you settle for less because you feel inferior? Learn how to ask for what you deserve and think about what you'd do if the consequences didn't matter. Then go and do it.

You can do it!

February 9th

If we neglect our garden weeds will grow. Over time our garden will have wild plants bursting through the soil with no order. Similarly, our brain is a garden where thoughts grow. Even if we are unaware of our thoughts or if we don't feel responsible for them they will pop up. If we don't practice conscious control over our thoughts we must understand that negative and distracting thoughts will come up. Often distracting and limiting thoughts contain seeds of fear and doubt. Fear is just like a weed growing in a neglected garden. Unintentional and unconscious thoughts are negative, wild and destructive. The ego in us does everything to protect itself. It bursts into an unbridled attack on everything that threatens it and often creates negative thoughts. The only way to prevent the outbursts is to consciously plant positive thoughts. You can do that by understanding that you are responsible for your thoughts. There's never a vacuum and we always have a thought in our mind so let's make sure it's positive.

Today be aware of and listen to your thoughts. Think positive thoughts.

I am sure miracles happen, even those we are unaware of.

February 10th

It's very easy to spend money, but earning it is a different story. Since childhood we are programmed to spend money on things we don't need, but feel we must have. If we calculated all the money that we have spent on worthless things then we would discover that we have spent more than we thought.

Let's learn how to save, as the poem *"A White Penny for a Black Day"* teaches us because what else can we do? Life is unstable and unpredictable. Medical developments have increased life expectancies, which requires us to think about saving at a young age. It's important to recognize the power of compound interest. Let's make a rule to save a fixed portion of our income each month for the rest of our lives. How much should we save? The minimum should be at least 10% of your monthly earnings, but one must decide the amount for themselves. If this concept is difficult then imagine that your workplace has reduced your income by 10%.

No matter how painful saving money may seem, it will serve you well in the long run. There are always going to be crises, stock market bubbles, wars, corruption, epidemics and God knows what else to empty your bank account. You must be on guard and keep your piggy bank full.

The rule of thumb is to invest a percentage of your income, which should be 100 minus your age, into the market. For example, if you are 40 years old, 100 - 40 is 60, so 60% of your savings should be invested. The rest should be invested in bonds. And no, don't be tempted to buy individual stocks. Buy funds that represent the current market indexes.

Open an investment account today even if you only have a small amount of money. The most important thing is that you make a monthly deposit!

February 11th

I always get excited by the power of thought.

It's the most powerful gift we have. I see it in myself as an experienced investment manager. When looking at market behavior in the short term it's random and often goes against logic. Right when it seemed like I had learned everything I encountered new situations. Randomness is an integral part of market behavior, which distills human desires into an aggregate investment decision.

At work I noticed how my mind delivers fresh solutions and ways of investing. If I tried to explain everything I would surely be hospitalized. But seriously, I'm endlessly thrilled with the creative solutions that my mind provides. It's just amazing that we all have this infinite power that has infinity neurons which make up an information network that finds solutions to our problems.

Think of a problem that is challenging and ask your mind for a solution. It will show up, give it time. Mighty forces are working behind the scenes to provide you with an answer. Your job is to wait patiently. It will appear at the right time.

February 12th

We don't always see the end, but if we do we become afraid and stop moving.

When I started writing this book I didn't say "I need at least 365 insights. It's going to be impossible." I just trusted my vision and let the road lead me. Step by step this book began to take shape while my personal goal was to write more pages. I can say with complete confidence that I grew by writing this book. I have been happier and more peaceful, no matter the circumstances. I'm thrilled by the miracle of life and I now desire to do good and influence positively. My cynicism has given way to acceptance, and my compassion, optimism, and gratitude has become infinite!

.

February 13th

Where there is doubt there is fear. The question is, what are you going to do about it?

Do you let fear be at the front and center stage? Does the tragic duo of doubt and fear fuel your drama? Whose authority do they have to steal your thunder? Yours. Why do you give so much power to these emotions that go beyond their necessary roles?! This is the opposite of what you want. It's your duty to return these emotions to their places. Keep the frontstage for courage and hope so that the play runs harmoniously. Let doubt and fear remain in the shadows where they belong.

Courage and hope are forces for tremendous change and motivation. Give them the respect they deserve. Unlike doubt and fear, the treacherous two, courage and hope will serve you faithfully. Don't forget for a moment that you are the director of your life. Choose your cast of emotions carefully and consciously. The success of your play will depend on your choices.

February 14th

Valentine's Day.

Today is Valentine's Day.

But what exactly is love?

Love begins with us. It's first accepting ourselves unconditionally. Love is learning to accept that we have flaws and that we are human.

Loving others is accepting them the way they are right now and not the way we want them to be. Love is accepting others even if we don't completely understand them, because who fully understands their selves or motives?

Today is an opportunity to practice love.

First, let's remind ourselves that we love ourselves because there is no reason not to! After all, we are with ourselves all the time even when we go to sleep, so we need to care about loving ourselves!

Second, today is an opportunity to thank someone in our life. Even if it's only thanking me for writing this book, that's okay! Just thank someone!

The most important thing to remember is love doesn't cost money. Money is just a tool you can use sometimes to express your love. Give special attention to someone close to you. Remind them in words, hugs or actions that you love them.

February 15th

Failure is not an option.
This is a powerful phrase and can create a life full of power and self-fulfillment. I first heard this phrase when a successful Israeli mentor was interviewed. The interview focused on the circumstances of his life and his tremendous way of overcoming them. He was asked, "What would have happened if you failed?" He replied, "Failure is not an option."

Do you live this way as well? What happens when we run into failure? We can treat failure in a positive way by looking at it as an opportunity in disguise. Failure is a natural part of growth and it teaches us about ourselves. Most people see failure as a negative thing, the fear of failure prevents them from trying and realizing their dreams in the first place. What happens if you try and fail? Well, you've tried and failed, but more importantly you didn't fail to try.

February 16th

One of my favorite books that I loved reading to my daughters was Dr. Seuss's Oh, the Places You'll Go!

Dr. Seuss has been ridiculed by publishers for his ideas and books. He chose to ignore them. Instead, he listened to his inner voice that guided him to fulfill his vision. In his book, the line "Kid, you'll move mountains" stood out to me in particular. Each and every one of us is the same kid who can move mountains. It's sad that we've stopped believing in that.

There's also a story about a baby elephant in a circus trying to reach freedom. The little elephant tried with all his might to free himself from the pole that held him captive, but he was without success. At some point he gave up and never tried again. Over the years the baby elephant became an adult weighing as much as a truck. It was still tied to the same shabby pole that, with a slight pull, could be torn right out of the ground. However, the belief that he couldn't do it was stronger than his physical power, and that's what keeps him tied to the pole.

You too are grown up. What are your limiting beliefs that keep you tied to the same old pole from childhood?

February 17th

I often talk about the importance of spiritual growth.

Most of us spend too much time on our external image and abandon our more important inner-self. Some of us spend a lot of money and resources cultivating our exterior image while unintentionally neglecting the interior. Spiritual growth incorporates holistic vision and considers the external image as well; a healthy and whole mind will inevitably radiate outwards. Spiritual growth allows us to grow internally. In other words, spiritual growth allows us to choose our thoughts, feelings and actions. We must learn that who we are doesn't depend on external circumstances, but stems from internal harmony. Life isn't able to stop us from self-fulfillment.

Make time for spiritual growth every day. Even just a few minutes of meditation, deep breathing, or talking to yourself with kind words or telling yourself that you love yourself is a good place to start!

February 18th

Our pursuit of happiness has become a weapon for the advertising industry.

We are constantly bombarded with messages that ask us to purchase more and more; more vacations, more gadgets, more debt. But it isn't the products or vacations that we so desperately need, it's happiness. You can go on your dream vacation and buy that latest phone that you don't really need, but negative feelings will eventually arrive and like an addict you will need to buy more and more things to maintain your "happiness".

This is how many good people find themselves enslaved in the endless pursuit for the next experience or product. This sure isn't the recipe for happiness it was portrayed to be. This is a recipe for bankruptcy as consumption sometimes requires loans whose payments can take years with its interest rates that slowly climb, all for that momentary sense of happiness that has long ended.

February 19th

Sometimes we find ourselves endlessly preparing for something, but still don't feel ready to take action.
It could be an idea that you've always wanted to try such as opening a store or taking a trip to the other side of the globe. The inner fire grips you and you're full of adrenaline and a desire to devour the world. But there may be opposing forces within you. You have the goal of moving forward, but it's also scary to leave your comfort zone. Then you have those closest to you telling you how impossible what you want to do is and push you to give up and get back to reality. That is their experience and their opinion. What is your opinion? Where is your fire? Don't let feelings of fear paralyze you, you deserve more than that. Allow yourself to break boundaries. The sky's the limit for some, but not for you! The vision in your mind can be real, it's up to you to manifest it into reality.

Don't stop and push against fear. You'll reach new places, stunning places, I promise!

February 20th

American theologian Reinhold Niebuhr (1892-1971) composed a prayer of peace. An abbreviated version was adopted by rehab organizations, the most famous one being Alcoholics Anonymous. It incorporates it as its motto for its twelve-step program. I've chosen to share the prayer today. Think about memorizing the first 7 lines as they contain the essence of personal responsibility.

> *"God grant me the serenity*
> *To accept the things I cannot change;*
> *Courage to change the things I can;*
> *And wisdom to know the difference.*
> *Living one day at a time;*
> *Enjoying one moment at a time;*
> *Accepting hardships as the pathway to peace;*
> *Taking, as He did, this sinful world*
> *As it is, not as I would have it;*
> *Trusting that He will make things right*
> *If I surrender to His Will;*
> *So that I may be reasonably happy in this life*
> *And supremely happy with Him*
> *Forever and ever in the next."*

I've nothing else to add, just Amen!

February 21th

There is nothing in the world like a mother's love. Sometimes it's so strong it's suffocating, but it's never a mother's fault. It's in her nature to ferociously care for her children.

Yes, I know, at times mothers can be a burden. They can interfere too much and we just want to get away from them!

There's nothing wrong with that, it's natural.

They say that one mother is enough to care for 5 children. However, 5 children can't take care of one mother.

Take a look at your relationship with your mother, or with your parents in general. They tried (in their own way and with their own perspectives) to share their experiences with you and teach you about the possibilities of life. Remember that your parents are victims of victims. When you become a parent you will hear your parents' voices and words coming out of your own mouth.

So, before it's too late take advantage of this day, cherish your mother. Talk to her, hug her, look at her and say thank you!

(And of course, don't forget your father).

February 22th

Let's make the impossible possible.

This isn't a cliché, but a motto I've created for myself when I was recently supposed to receive a shipment of porcelain pomegranates for a relative who was visiting me in Israel. They were staying for a short time and had to take off in a few days. When shipping said it was going to be late, I contacted the manufacturer through their website to check why there was a delay. It turned out that due to a malfunction the package hadn't even shipped. The manufacturing company has offered to compensate me by adding two slightly different pomegranates. It was a fair offer and from their point of view they felt like they had compensated me for my trouble.

I instinctively tend to accept these kinds of solutions rather than argue, but this time it wasn't me who wanted this package, it was my relative! It was better to have one pomegranate for my aunt who was overseas than two pomegranates for myself. So, I thought about how to make this impossible possible.

I contacted the manufacturer again and told them the whole ordeal and suggested that they convert the compensation of two extra pomegranates to a faster delivery by courier. They agreed and we both came out the other end satisfied. This was a situation in which I haven't let the circumstances determine what was possible. I'm giving this example because it shows how I was able to achieve desirable results even with the little things in life. Since then, I've practiced making the impossible possible to achieve my desired results regardless of the circumstance.

I always ask, "How can I make the impossible possible?" Try it for yourself and see the amazing results you'll get. Try it at the first opportunity you get and then give yourself a pat on the back when you succeed.

February 23th

I believe that we live in two parallel universes.
From the moment we are born who we truly are disappears. We get divided by society, family, friends and work. We are constantly silenced and crammed into societal boxes that forces us to give up our true identities, desires and everything else that sets us apart from others. From infancy we're assimilated into codes of conduct and desires that are appropriate to our culture. Over time our souls seek ways to express themselves. Consciousness, curiosity and truth search for the real and authentic. Nurture it, it's happiness and your true desire. It's the one and only you.

It's true that you'll need a lot of courage and willingness to break conventions but your comfort zone is causing a lot of suffering. It will become unbearable and more miserable than your fears. Break the chains that bind you and search for self-fulfillment. Allow consciousness, curiosity and truth to guide, you will be rewarded.

February 24th

Let's start with a joke.

There was someone who wanted to win the lottery so badly that he decided to turn to God. Every night before he went to bed he fervently prayed to God to let him win the lottery so that he could live the life he had always wanted. The message eventually reached the angels who were in charge of fulfilling dreams. They approached God at their annual meeting and told God that there was someone who was praying for a long time and with determination. God told the angel that he was noticed, but couldn't help him since he hadn't bought a single lottery ticket.

You see, sometimes we are dreaming about something for so long that we forget to start taking action. Start with small steps, or what I like to call confidence-building steps. Your dream will slowly begin to come true, but you must first wake up.

Are you awake?

February 25th

In recent decades finances have become so sophisticated that making money has become a real work of art. We can make money just by the press of a button by taking out a loan and suddenly having a tremendous amount of money in our accounts. However, this comes with a lot of consequences. We're constantly bombarded by advertisements that prey on our desires. Their purpose of course is for us to buy their products. Even if you don't have money, it's not a problem, just take out a loan or use a credit card. Get what you want at all costs.

But someone needs to repay that loan, and that someone is going to be on you. You'll be repaying that loan long after you've forgotten the experience that you used it for. Is it worth it, tying up your future in debt for momentary pleasure? I'm not saying that you shouldn't participate in consumption, just have balance with it. Taking out a loan for emotional pleasure is just enslaving you to debt.

Try to limit yourself and spend less than you earn. You'll gain peace of mind, better sleep and financial security over time.

February 26th

Savings. Yes, savings.

A small part of your income should go to savings so that over the years you will accumulate a significant amount of money. Wouldn't you be happy if you had some financial security?

Do you have enough income to save? The standard of living has increased significantly in recent decades. The amount of money each family or individual earns is noticeably higher than in recent decades and yet, many fail to make ends meet. Do you think that if your income doubles or triples you'll then reach economic well-being? According to statistics, despite the rise in wages, many won't have any money left over at the end of the month. Miraculously, expenses exceed income. It seems like a lost race. Who decides all this? You and only you.

I know it's hard, but there are bad financial practices you must unlearn. Make it a habit to save a specific amount of money or a percentage of your income every month. Imagine that what you put aside isn't yours and you can't use it. It then has a chance to grow. For example, if you deposit $100 in a mutual fund or ETF that tracks the US Central Stock Index the annual yield history is close to 10% per year. If you put this amount in every month, regardless of what is happening to the stock market and the drama that unfolds on tv, after 10 years you will have about $20,000. What happens if you keep saving and don't touch it for 30 years, The amount approaches $200,000, a respectable sum by all accounts.

Do you see how small sums of money can easily become huge? Start with something small. Save for future financial peace. Start today!

February 27th

Say thank you and practice gratitude humbly from the heart.
This is one of the best things you can do for yourself. With gratitude you can become more confident because you can see and appreciate your achievements. You can take away your competitive spirit which just makes you compare yourself to others anyways. You can give recognition to your actions and achievements. These are your accomplishments, be proud of them!

No one can take these things away from you. Take pride in yourself!

February 28th

What makes you feel depressed?
Is it your economic or familial situation? Are the government's decisions making you anxious? I don't judge people for failing to retain composure in situations of great difficulty (such as death, divorce, etc). In most cases, the depression that so many of us have become addicted to doesn't depend on the circumstances (except in extreme clinical cases). Everything is usually physically fine. You're no different from others, your level of security and income are rising, even your life expectancy is rising! Depression stems from the gap of what we desire and what we have. This gap won't ever close, even if you're earning shoot up like crazy. The gap is inevitable, we'll always want more than what we have. That's the human condition.

Do you exist in abundance or scarcity? Minimalism or consumerism? During the 2008 financial crisis an acquaintance of mine told me about his friend who was worth hundreds of millions of dollars. However, during the crisis he lost a most of his money and he wanted to commit suicide. Some of us would have been happy to swap lives with him because after all he still had tens of millions of dollars left, but the average person's dream doesn't feel the same for the billionaire's nightmare.

It's not the circumstances that make you feel a certain way, but your attitude. It's judgment that causes our emotions. See life as a miracle. Money doesn't cure its ailments. Choose to feel good, it's your choice!

February 29th

Many times our fear of failure paralyzes us. But why look at fear this way?

A better way to look at fear is to transform it into curiosity. We will then focus on learning and enthusiasm. The outcome is less threatening and we feel freedom from the crushing fear.

What an amazing way to live.

March

March 1ˢᵗ

A little bit about happiness

Everyone wants to be happy, it's universal. There are many books on happiness and how to achieve it. I believe that reading or researching other ways to achieve happiness serves as a catalyst to being happier. Therefore, happiness solely depends on us and not the external world. Are kids playing soccer on turf less happy than the kids surrounded by piles of luxurious material goods? Is the rich person who spends his day at work happier than the poor person who lives in a straw hut in front of a wild landscape, but never leaves it? I don't think so! Happiness doesn't depend on your surroundings, but only on you and your perception, approach to life, and the challenges and difficulties you must face in order to live that life.

One should practice being happy no matter the circumstance. It's hard to constantly choose happiness, but with time it becomes second nature. If you take responsibility for your happiness then you will be happier. Inner power and peace comes from taking responsibility over your own happiness, and not letting other people or circumstances affect it.

Today, accept what is and change what you can. Forgive what doesn't matter!

March 2nd

The biggest mistake you can make is to not make mistakes.
A mistake helps significantly in the process of growth. Mistakes allow us to learn, improve and adjust our sites on the right solution. He who doesn't do, doesn't make mistakes. In modern society mistakes are often given much more weight than they deserve. A mistake can get intertwined with self-image and is then perceived as something unworthy and even unforgivable. It's understandable when it happens during an open heart surgery, but in fact, even the most skilled doctors make mistakes.

Mistakes are inevitable, it's part of being human. Large corporations often sink by searching for scapegoats instead of searching for solutions. It's acceptable and satisfies the immediate appetite of the "angry mob" that searches for someone to blame when something doesn't work. And if that means firing the CEO then even better! This is the sinful part of blame that turns human behavior into something reproachful and condemnatory because once you're finished with this problem another one pops up. Therefore, instead of punishing people for mistakes one should accept another's faults with compassion and know that one can learn from failures and grow from it.

Learn to forgive yourself and others for the things you can't control. Learn the lessons as they are offered and remember that it's only human to make mistakes.

March 3rd

If we really want to get to the root of things you have to ask why.

As a child this question was casually asked. If we were not given a satisfactory answer then we'd ask again and again until we reached the core answer. Children are the ones guided by will and truth. As sophisticated adults we've learned to disguise our feelings, desires and even ourselves. Just asking "why" can reveal a world full of hidden motives, repression and avoidances. A common example is the fear of making a change in the workplace. "Why do I keep going to work if I am just suffering there? Because it's convenient for me, I have seniority and everyone knows me. I'm comfortable because the salary is good and I can support my family." What does that actually mean? "I'm afraid that I won't succeed elsewhere and that my quality of life will decrease. So, I will force myself to suffer for this job."

Is it worth it? Definitely not! Life is short, one day it will end so why settle for little? Why?

March 4ᵗʰ

Learn to forgive yourself.

You have made and will make mistakes. Someday you'll probably embarrass yourself and those around you. Maybe you'll stand in front of an audience and have a slip of the tongue, you'll hiccup, or God forbid, unintentionally share the perfumed scent your bottom produces. Maybe you'll say something stupid in a ridiculous way, maybe you'll fall down the stairs onto your butt, step in gum or dog poo. In fact, the possibilities for embarrassment are endless. Why do we need to punish ourselves for that? It's human and statistically these events will definitely happen to all of us. It's okay, nothing happened, the sky didn't fall. Look up, it doesn't seem like the stars are interested in the stupid things we've done. So why not just forgive ourselves? This isn't an unusual endeavor and at any given time someone in the world is experiencing the same thing... It isn't a big deal. Forgive yourself and move on.

March 5th

Today we will focus on breathing.

This basic action, though natural and barely perceptible, occurs from the second we are born until the second we surrender back to our creator. Breathing offers a powerful element of healing, an almost magical power that can change a mood. It can bring awareness and recharge someone with positive energy in a short span of time.

There are 1,440 minutes in a day. Pause at least once a day for one minute and dedicate that time to yourself. For one minute practice relaxation by breathing deeply and slowly through your nose. Close your eyes and focus on your breathing. Inhale through your nose, fill your lungs with air, and exhale through your nose. Repeat a few times and see your thoughts slow, your body relax, and your vitality increase.

If you find another free minute out of the 1,440 minutes try it again.

March 6th

What's important is what I think of myself!

Depression has become an epidemic. The excessive use of multiple medications wouldn't be necessary if we weren't overly-concerned with what we think about ourselves. It seems that many of us have decided to hand others the keys to our self-esteem. Our self-esteem is influenced by what others think about us or expect from us instead of what we think of or expect from ourselves.

It starts immediately from infancy with the loving care of your parents. It continues when you're handed over to external caregivers who, with scrutinizing eyes, categorize you as a difficult baby, one who doesn't sleep and wakes everyone up. It continues with teachers and educators who are worried by your cognitive abilities and are quick to put a label on you. The results of your exams have determined the degree of your intelligence. This continues in your career when you long for words of approval and appreciation from your employer. It will never end unless you make it end

Is it logical to allow others to control us this way? The answer is absolutely not! Only we have the right and responsibility to decide who we are. What others think of us is ultimately not our business! We must develop a way to think independently. We must rely on ourselves, knowing that only we can choose the best goals for ourselves and only we can develop the strength to ignore the negative things that others have told us! Only then we will truly achieve independence and freedom. When we're responsible for our thoughts and destiny we are our masters!

Remember this today as you interact with others. Practice transforming negative thoughts others have about you into healthy thoughts full of compassion.

Remove those heavy chains and reap the benefits of freedom!

March 7th

It is recommended, and even required, that we make mistakes. Mistakes often cause us embarrassment. Our image falls apart in front of others when we make mistakes, but the fact is that perfection only exists in existing at all. Any growth in our lives will always be accompanied by mistakes. The only person who never makes mistakes is the one who doesn't do anything at all. Make as many mistakes as you must, this is how you'll learn and grow. The idea is to not repeat the same mistake twice, because then the lesson obviously hasn't been learned. As the saying goes, "The one who doesn't learn from history is doomed to relive it again and again." Mistakes are priceless because they help us better adjust. Mistakes teach us what to watch out for, how to prepare, and how to use alternative ways to achieve results.

Think about this today. Forgive yourself and allow yourself to make mistakes because you deserve it.

Don't be afraid and don't hesitate. In every mistake there are seeds of success.

Good luck!

March 8th

"There's not a thing that stands in the way of what you desire."

This is a well-known proverb in Judaism. There is great power in internalizing it.

Our will has its own power and if we understand that then we can harness it.

The phenomenon of phantom pregnancy is great at illustrating the power of desire and its ability to create reality. During phantom pregnancy the woman experiences every symptom a pregnant woman does even though she is not pregnant. Her heart's tremendous desire to experience motherhood creates a fantasy pregnancy for her body. The symptoms are the same, the sensations are similar, however, it's not a real pregnancy. The mind just strongly believed in it! Amazing!

The will's power has the ability to create a reality that will hit us like a strike of lighting. In order to learn how to use this power we must ask ourselves what we truly want. Once we have clarified that we can tune in and use the power in our favor. To use our will's power we must focus on only one thing.

Be aware of your thoughts and think of what is most important to you. Choose one thing and concentrate. Start to harness your power of desire when you feel it inside you, let it work for you.

March 9th

Each of us has a hero we identify with and admire, but they provide us with unattainable desires. The hero symbolizes ideals we strive for that often seem unachievable through human behaviors such as courage, mortality, wealth and love.

To some of us, these desires seemed ideal before we tried to implement them. It's enough to take a small step each day since life is about growth and growth doesn't always come quick. On the contrary, it's actually a slow process. But by taking one step at a time we become smarter and more experienced. The pursuit of our dreams makes us better versions of ourselves. The road often seems far away and unattainable, but a journey of a thousand miles begins with one small step. The most important thing is perseverance and the belief that we don't need to be perfect.

Today look at your hero and think of a characteristic they have that you would like to adopt and go for it without need for perfection.

March 10th

Night reading:

It's time to say a prayer. Today is over and it's time to go to bed. Tomorrow is another day and there will be new opportunities so it doesn't matter if today was successful or not. It's over. You're still here on earth and no one knows that yesterday didn't go well. Let go of all your worries and release the bad thoughts. Breathe deeply and say a short prayer from the depths of your heart.

Thank God, your family and your friends for being with you. Thank yourself for who you are, empty your mind and focus on your breathing.

Breathe in slowly. Feel the air come in through your nose, filling your stomach, and imagine that tomorrow will be a happy day.

Good night and see you tomorrow morning.

March 11th

We don't have to understand everything, whether it's work, school, finances, family, etc.
Not understanding something isn't a sign of inferiority or a lack of professionalism, knowledge grows in a geometric progression. Every year the rate of information doubles so it's impossible to know everything. Information on the micro and nano level makes it possible to slowly understand the most basic elements like DNA, the structure of the atom, etc.

Today, I invite you to get rid of the burden that you'll never know everything, and that's fine. This shouldn't prevent you from learning. Allow yourself to enjoy being human and feel lucky to be living in a time when the amount of information is so tremendous. Don't expect yourself to know everything. Prevent disappointment. Everything is fine!

March 12th

Do not be afraid of disappointing.

At some point you'll disappoint someone. Most of us are so eager to please and avoid negative judgments that we change our behavior. We tend to dismiss ourselves, our inner voice, and the compass that directs our lives through our values. Many times we disappoint the most important person in our lives- ourselves.

It's impossible to please everyone. For me, I tell those disappointed with me to "Take a number and stand in line." The line is long and that's okay. There are too many people and too many things to do that trying to please everyone will not help improve myself or my spiritual growth. So, for me I'm okay with my decision to let others be disappointed in me.

Make sure your actions serve your values, beliefs and potential. You'll be judged by others no matter what, but that's their problem. Don't disappoint yourself by pleasing others!

March 13th

Albert Einstein once said, "It's not that I'm so smart, I just stay with problems longer."

We're intelligent beings. The brain makes up about 2% of your weight. Despite its lightness, it consumes about 20% of our oxygen. Our brain uses the energy for countless things. For example, we have about 60,000 thoughts every day. That's about one second per thought.

Conscious thinking is the best activity someone can do for themselves. Everything starts with a thought. I'm sure you've come across the concept "perception creates reality." So if you want something, the best thing you can do is to consciously think about it. The brain produces about 60,000 thoughts per day (most of them unconscious) so it's enough that only 1 out of every 1000 thoughts are what we want to consciously think about. That would give us about 60 new conscious thoughts a day about things that are important to us.

You are what you think. Think about it. You will have 60,000 thoughts a day no matter what.

March 14th

"Know thyself."
Socrates.

What is there to know? What about ourselves do we not know? What we do know is probably the tip of the iceberg. What do I really want? What are my abilities? What's special about me? What are my advantages and disadvantages? What motivates me? And what controls me? Who am I actually?

Know yourself; it's an ongoing and constantly changing process because we too are changing and growing. "Know thyself" allows you to break boundaries. As children we were constantly engaged with this. We took on challenges, studied different subjects, learned to ride bikes, ran around, discovered our talents such as painting, singing, etc.

What are you doing today to get to know yourself better? Consistent exploration will allow you to see what's motivating you. Once you understand yourself you can take responsibility for your thoughts, which will eventually become reality.

March 15th

Do you believe in God?

Faith takes many forms. We yearn to believe that there's something watching from above and protecting us. We want to believe that our existence has meaning and that we'll continue to exist after death in some way or another. It doesn't matter which god you believe in, faith is powerful. Belief in God means you have belief in yourself. God is embodied through you; man was created in the image of God, therefore there is a divine spark in you.

Respect yourself, forgive yourself, love yourself and have faith in God.

March 16th

What is your point of view?

Sometimes we have the tendency to blame external forces for our circumstances. For example, we can explain why we change jobs so much- our bosses abuse us so we therefore have no choice but to be constant victims and doomed to wander between jobs.

In this case there's nothing we can do since everything is predetermined. It's a passive approach that puts blame on an external thing. Is this what will make us grow? Why not take responsibility for our own destiny? True, there are circumstances that we can't change, but how we respond is our responsibility and is the one that makes the difference.

If we learn how to control our reactions, we'll become responsible. We can act to change things. Pass the baton to yourself and awaken your awareness of your inner attribution. Is the reason why many people change jobs like socks really dependent on the boss's behavior? Or is it due to our behavior; a lack of seriousness, contempt, fatigue?

Internal attribution allows us to explore and ask ourselves, is there anything I can do to improve the situation?

March 17th

Passivity has its great qualities, among them is giving others control over our lives.

When something or someone else is responsible for us it takes away the burden of dealing with anything. On the other hand, it creates physical and mental dependence. Growth is done through resistance. It's a law of nature that we must recognize. In order to grow we must break the boundaries we've created for ourselves, after that the sky is the limit. Our self-limitation keeps us from moving forward. It can't be seen and sometimes disguises itself as fear. The crippling fear weaves cobwebs around us and traps us in a false reality.

It's time to change your mindset and move towards action because if you don't someone else will do it for you.

March 18th

What's the question?

What do you ask yourself in different situations?

When you ask "what's going to happen?" you're asking a passive question, which moves the responsibility off of you. You're left without protection, since then the outcome depends on the circumstances and not the actions you take.

Asking "what can I do" is an empowering question that puts you in the driver's seat. You then have the best chance of getting what you want. Be the captain. It's hard and scary, but it's rewarding and the right thing to do!

So, what can you do?

March 19th

Ask for what you deserve.

Do you think that there are not enough resources on this planet and you must therefore be content with little? Are you doomed to live in deprivation because that's how it is and there's not enough? We're stardust, there is more than enough to satisfy everyone's needs. Most of us haven't had the privilege of being born with silver spoons in our mouths. Most of us are forced to roll up our sleeves and deal with things. It isn't a bad thing, it's how it is. In the modern age there's possibility for development and growth, independently and rapidly like never before in human history. The availability of information, its accessibility and the ability to reach tens of thousands of people at the click of a button allows every individual to achieve things that were once exclusive to emperors.

Ask for what you deserve in the world without fear or shame. There's enough for everyone. You deserve it.

March 20th

March 20th – International Day of Happiness.
In a calendar that marks special days happiness merits its own space! Bringing happiness into awareness is an important act. At the end of our journey, we'll discover that everybody has been looking for it all along! We strive for money, success, health and hedonistic pleasures all with the goal of improving our happiness. Happiness must accompany us every moment as it's an experience worth living for. On this day the awareness for happiness exists on a collective level, which is a good opportunity for us to stop and think for a minute. Are the things that we're doing truly making us happy? If not, then what does and why don't we do more of it?

Many of the things that we associate happiness with were fed to us in a relatively harmful way. We are going to feel happy only if we buy this item or that piece of clothing (along the way we'll go bankrupt, but that doesn't matter). And what is success? Does it hold the key to happiness? Or does happiness lead to success? I tend to believe that happiness leads us to our successes. Happy people are usually positive and as a result feel energetic and confident in their day-to-day lives. They're sending a clear message to the universe regarding themselves and their goals. It's then absorbed by us who like and are attracted to optimistic, curious, energetic people. We want to be in their presence.

So, what do we need to do to be happy? Simply and humbly accept what there is. Our lives were started miraculously, they shouldn't be taken for granted.

Stop, look around, breathe deeply and say thank you. It's up to you, *not* the circumstances!

March 21th

Never in human history has personal potential been so high as the present.
The age in which we live has high levels of potential personal growth that didn't exist before. The number of professions to choose from is tremendous and the flexibility with which we can change our careers or gain new abilities is unimaginable. Everywhere people are reinventing themselves. You hear amazing stories about people who have quickly created their wealth. The options are endless, but it takes a lot of self-discipline, a plan of action and courage. I don't say these things in ignorance, in the United States alone there are over 1,700 new millionaires per day. This is a rate of less than one minute per new millionaire. Every year in the United States over half a million millionaires are "born"! There has never been a time like this in history when people became rich at these rates.

You carry a tremendous resource- your mind. Use it. Thinking consciously is the best thing you can do for yourself. You can do it. The excuses are over!

March 22th

The gap between the existing and the desirable is the biggest obstacle to success.
In itself it isn't an obstacle at all. But often, instead of concentrating on the actions we need to close the gap, we're busy cultivating unhappiness. We lament our bitter fate, if only we had the ability or the resources we needed we could have succeeded. Reality is more complex than that. Successful people understand that there's a gap between the ideal situation and the reality they have now. They are constantly working to find solutions and improvise. They don't wait for the stars to align and they don't grumble or wait, they act with what they have.

A gap will always exist between what you are today and what you can be. It can create a lot of tension and resistance. Be aware of this and remember that you don't have to focus on the final goal, but just on each individual step. This is how you will progress and fend off fear. So get going and take the first step! Everything will work out, don't worry you will succeed!

March 23th

Where's the focus?

Focus needs to be like a laser beam, accurate and powerful. It can be extremely powerful. Are you focusing on reading this or is your focus elsewhere? Learn to control what you focus on. It will allow the thing you're focused on to manifest, whether it's good or bad. Usually when we aren't aware of this our focus diminishes and we don't achieve what we want (sometimes the opposite of what we desire occurs).

Focus on what makes you feel good. Focus on your growth... Now.

March 24th

Humankind creates their own life, no one creates it for them. But that's not enough. They should, after creating their life, also choose it, and recognize that it's the best life for them.

I train myself to see how beautiful the life I've created for myself is. It's the only way I can reach deep peace. Wanting to live someone else's life is destructive. To want the life that might have been mine if I were more or less X, if I had this or that, if I was born not here but there is a waste of time and a waste of a life. Only live your life.

Be content with yourself and recognize that you're a miracle. You're in charge of your life. Only you!

March 25th

Life is dynamic.
Change is constant, and that's what scares us. Even if we are stagnant, the environment around us still changes. We must recognize that this is the law of nature. Change doesn't distinguish between good and bad. It's not for or against us. It's just change. So, why don't we initiate change? There's no doubt that it's scary since change might be outside of our comfort zone where the familiar and safe are. Eventually though, this area becomes uncomfortable and starts to make us miserable.

Change that you've initiated will allow you to develop and grow. You may sometimes feel like you've made a mistake, but remember that people regret the things that they didn't do, not the things they did.

Create the habit of initiating change. Change will come either way so why not create it yourself?

March 26ᵗʰ

Change.
It keeps happening. It's dynamic and it's part of life. It's not actively working against you, it's simply how the universe works. Galaxies are born and galaxies fade, suns die and one day it will happen to our solar system as well. Change is essential to our universe. We must welcome it. We too are constantly changing, and so is our environment, friends, family, neighborhood, city and country. We must accept it. Fear of change is fear of the unknown. Our need to cling to the familiar is sometimes so strong that it blinds us to other possibilities.

Almost always change is for the better. Even if at first sight change seems to be bad for us, eventually we will learn and grow from it. Muscles are built from resistance, running improves by effort, cognitive abilities improve by strenuous thinking and change allows us to grow our potential. The difficulty that comes with change will build character and strength.

Commit to change, it's inevitable and can do tremendous things for us.

March 27th

Think about our reactions to situations; are we automatically reacting or are we consciously choosing how we want to react? Have we invested thought in it? Have you ever wondered about your behavior? We press on the brakes and the accelerator automatically because we've practiced it tens of thousands of times. But should autopilot be in other aspects of our lives? Should we give it control over our reactions? We are all familiar with these automatic behaviors that sometimes hurt us. We've all encountered a situation where someone we love says something offensive that automatically causes us to react with insult, anger or revenge.

Is this really what we want or do past events, childhood memories or similar situations come up in that moment reviving those memories along with the fear, worthlessness and inferiority it comes with? Does it really have a place in the present?

This isn't an easy challenge, but we still have to take responsibility and change our reactions into growth-oriented reactions. Are there people who react differently and in a more constructive way? Of course! So choose not to be offended because there's no reason to really. You're not responsible for the thoughts of others. Choose not to get angry or upset and instead choose to trust yourself. Believe in yourself and your ability to grow. There's no reason to act otherwise. You will be happier.

Consciously manage your reactions and let autopilot drive you home.

March 28th

Be grateful.
In recent years there has been progress in the study of happiness, which is different from what was being studied at the beginning of the 20th century. The focus used to be on trying to find the source of pain. Talking through childhood and healing oneself was long, difficult and often discouraging. Happiness was luxurious.

Today the trend is shifting towards spiritual growth, personal empowerment and the pursuit of happiness. One of the fastest ways to become happier is practicing gratitude. With gratitude we understand that nothing is to be taken for granted. Sometimes we think that excessive consumption of material items makes us happier. Happiness does come up, but it's an illusion that depends on external actions. We first feel a burst of happiness and then a downfall. Like addicts we start rampantly shopping again or take medication or God forbid drugs. But we have an effective tool for happiness at our disposal, gratitude.

Be grateful every day for a few moments. Be grateful for yourself and for who you are. Be grateful for your family, your health, friends, etc. Don't wait for something to be taken from you to make you appreciate it. There's no point in waiting for someone's funeral to praise them, cherish them right now in their shortcomings and strengths. They are just a human being and like you they're also looking for happiness.

Practice gratitude in the morning and at night before bed. Make it a ritual or part of your routine. I appreciate you and wish you a wonderful life.

March 29th

Never listen to those who say no.
You know those people, maybe you're even one of them from time to time. It's not out of bad intentions of course, you want to protect those close to you from doing "crazy" things which can result in discouragement, failure or disappointment. You don't want to see your loved ones shattered by a failed dream just like your relatives don't want to see it happen to you.

There are tips however that worked for top notch successful people. Arnold Schwarzenegger used it in his plan for success. His whole life he has heard "no". As a teenager when he wanted to go into bodybuilding his family advised against it. He was from Austria and bodybuilding belonged to the Americans and British. Despite that he won bodybuilding competitions 13 times. Then he wanted to go into the American film industry. Think about how many times he heard the word "no" with his monstrous body and strange thick accent in the '70s. There was no place for someone like him, and yet one of the most memorable phrases in American cinema is "I'll be back" by Schwarzenegger with his heavy Austrian accent. Then to be governor of California, well really there's no chance- but yet again he heard the same inner voice that defied everyone else silently whispering in his ear "yes, yes, you can".

I ask you to focus on how against all odds a man managed to fulfill the impossible by listening to his inner voice that said "everything is possible." What about you? Everything is possible for you too!

March 30th

Look for inspiration.
Today it's easier than ever. In fact, it's in the palm of your hand. The technological revolution has made information available in every corner of the globe. Not for nothing there's the saying, "The world is in the palm of your hands." Smartphones make it possible to perform actions that many years ago were impossible without physically going to an office or mall. Whether it's at the doctor's, the post office, a government office, a traffic jam or a train ride it's not a rare sight to see a smartphone in almost every hand.

We choose to watch movies, play games, surf the web or just kill time, but why not make the habit of turning your device into an ally? This will give you more value. I ask that you create a small habit; everyday spend a few minutes watching, listening or reading about empowerment. There are a lot of YouTube channels that have inspirational motivational speech videos. Listen to powerful music or to a podcast on topics that interest you. You don't have to do it all the time, but the more you're aware of what's out there and are exposed to them, the more your happiness and serenity will steadily increase.

Do it, at most you'll be happier!

March 31th

We can always find someone to blame.
But, are we interested in that? Sure, we have a momentary feeling of relief, but the damage done far outweighs the short-term benefit. Finding a guilty party allows your ego to feel good about itself, but is there room for this when trying to achieve personal and spiritual growth? Definitely not! We must understand and recognize that we won't always get what we want or we won't always be completely understood. Disappointment will come from time to time. From a spiritual perspective blaming others is a waste of time and energy.

So, what do you do instead? As in any situation we take responsibility for our feelings and thoughts and recognize that the best way to find a solution is to not blame others, but to ask ourselves what we can do. As a result, the emotions will generate a new behavior that will produce the desired results.

April

April 1ˢᵗ - April Fool's Day

This day is a holiday for silly pranks. Big and productive companies, journalists and news anchors all fooling around and pranking each other. Notice how the seriousness, the severe facial expressions and the drama is so easily replaced with laughter and goodwill. We have a thirst for the lightness and wit that lacks in our daily lives. Society and social norms (which everyone agrees lacks a sense of humor) dictate that it's better to exist in a humorless rigid structure where people have to listen, behave and look serious. It goes against the balance and harmony that exists within everything. April Fool's Day serves as catharsis for all the playful and childish creativity trapped within us.

Set yourself free!

Take advantage of today and invite lightness and humor into your life. Prank your relatives, trick your friends and have fun with children by hiding candy. It's fun, it's liberating and the laughter that comes with the silliness is a natural part of our being. This day serves as a reminder to introduce humor and lightness into our lives whenever it's in our power. No need to wait for April 1st to fool around. You only live once and it would be a sad life if we forgot to laugh, joke around or be silly sometimes. You don't need to be so serious; life has a way of doing that for us.

April 2ⁿᵈ

In spite of everything there will always be setbacks.
Although you who read this book have consciously chosen the path of growth, sometimes the path asks you to stop or maybe even back up to see it more clearly. It's okay, that's life. Meditation, positive thinking, self-awareness and peaceful acceptance all make it possible to shorten the amount of time you struggle with your feelings. If you've managed to consciously lengthen the time period between "falls" and if you've also managed to shorten the length of time you stay down, pat yourself on the back. You're walking on the right path.

It's difficult to avoid bumps, but if we practice mindfulness then we'll have a longer "up" period. It's part of balance, just like there's no laughter without crying and no day without night, there is *no* success without failure.

So next time you feel down remember what Sir Winston Churchill said, "If you're going through Hell, keep going." And I'm adding, "the exit sign is just a little further down the road."

April 3rd

Some of us are experiencing depression.
As one of the most severe plagues in modern times, this major societal problem feeds pharmaceutical, herb, potion, workshop and guru industries who all swear that they can make you well. Why, in spite of all our abundance, does this mental illness bring down so many victims?

An old and fascinating study from the beginning of the last century examined the effect of what giving warmth and comfort to infants has on them. Orphans were divided into two groups. One received basic necessities as well as loving touch, soothing comfort and kind words. The second group was given only the basics to survive. The experiment had to be discontinued soon after it began because of disheartening results. The infants in the second group immediately declined physically and mentally... which led to infant mortality.

Think of all that we have today in our consumer culture. There is an infinite amount of products created to distract. This just leaves us feeling empty in our hearts and wallets. The dull pain that we experience can't be solved by another new shirt or phone. That's just an illusion and an addiction. We need warmth and love, and that isn't always guaranteed. The only cure for our distress is an ancient remedy that started from the beginning of humanity: belonging, family, unconditional love, warmth, love, hugs, kind words, and being present. It's the only real substitute for all the medicines and potions we take to cheer up.

Start the morning with a hug, a kind word or an authentic smile. Be grateful for who you are and the paths you've taken. Look in the mirror and smile at yourself. Have a lovely, lovely day.

April 4th

If there's one thing that people are willing to fight for, it's respect.
Disrespect is sometimes used as a pretext for war between countries. Politicians who send their people to die in war excite the masses through a need to restore respect. Family ties are severed due to violations of dignity, and there's no shortage of examples. What is this respect that so many are willing to sacrifice everything for? Respect is ultimately a need for recognition. A very basic need that hides in your stomach, a need that cries out, "I'm here, pay attention to me!"

Listen to children screaming, "Look at me!" This need doesn't disappear as we get older, it simply takes different forms. Everything we strive for as humans is respect in disguise. So let's practice giving respect so that we can improve our relationships.

We must internalize that everyone needs respect and giving it is very simple. Listening, eye contact, giving a sense of importance, smiling and understanding. Do that and see how your relationships improve miraculously. Do that now with every person you come in contact with, children, parents, professionals, friends, acquaintances, cashiers. Show them respect! Well done. Make them feel special. It will eventually come back to you!

April 5th

Let's make "risk" part of our lives.
We can choose to be on autopilot which would lead us to safe shores drama-free. The journey would be predictable and so would its ending. We could walk the path that is within our comfort zone, a path that doesn't have any surprises or contain much excitement, but what would be the point of spending a lifetime like that? Is that all? Is that what it's all about?

There's a battle within us between the creativity that wants to burst out and the automatic pilot that doesn't want us stirred up. The autopilot side controls us because it promises to fulfill our every need. Being on autopilot is not much better than believing you have control over reality. Believing this will only leave you frustrated and depressed with the feeling that someone else is controlling your life.

So jump into the front seat, hold the steering wheel, and watch for dead ends. And remember, you're the driver. This is how you reach other places. You'll expand boundaries and replace your frustration, depression and worthlessness with vitality, pride, and contentment. The improvement in your emotions will be immeasurable.

Like everything else, start with small steps. Consider whether or not you are living on autopilot. Consider taking full control every day for as long as you can and as long as you dare. Take risks and dare because the path does end. Make it meaningful and make it matter.

April 6th

Who are you living with right now?

Would you be willing to live with a person that tells you you're unsuccessful or that you won't amount to anything? What about a person whose despair is evident on their face and in their words, one who is both hopeless and useless? I sure hope not!

Our mind is a machine that constantly produces thoughts. Thoughts that float to the top are just the tip of the iceberg. We're governed by a collection of thoughts that touch on who we are, what our place in the world is, what we can and can't do and what we are good or bad at. Are these our thoughts?

There is no doubt that many of our thoughts were programmed into us as children. The mental software is mostly written by others and we act accordingly. Our thoughts are constant, good and bad, and often happen without our awareness. Our thoughts have a tremendous impact on our moods, happiness and perception.

Even when we assume we're not thinking thoughts still pop up. There is one basic important concept you must know: your mind is capable of examining only one thought at a time. Why not work on choosing which thought you want to entertain? The learning process can be long, but taking one step at a time will get you there. It's enough to replace even a small part of a negative thought with a thought that you've chosen for yourself. Making this correction will cause your happiness, self-confidence and compassion to grow. There's no doubt in my mind that your prize will be increased vitality and mood improvement.

Today be aware of your thoughts and make a conscious decision to replace all negative thoughts with positive ones. If you don't have something to replace your negative thoughts with, say "I love myself".

April 7th

Sometimes we find ourselves more or less responsible for the feelings of others. Sometimes we try to change their feelings, maybe improve their mood. Next, we identify with their unhappy feelings and absorb them as our own. This is how we end up exhausted and frustrated. It isn't our job to make someone else happy. Despite our great desire to help others this path will only lead to disappointment. The best way to help others is to show them compassion and inclusion. The best way to avoid drifting and sliding down the steep slope of someone else's emotions is by maintaining balance. It isn't our job to change another person's mood.

When you achieve balance and self-control you can be an example to others who seek your guidance. They don't admire you because you're a sponge who absorbed all of their negative feelings, but because you are a role model and a good example of how to react properly.

Today, carry this knowledge with you. Create self-balance and self-control. Please don't be a sponge for someone else. Leave the sponge in the kitchen where it belongs.

April 8th

So... what do I *really* want?

The thoughts we think throughout the day eventually manifest through our actions and behavior. There are no dull moments in our mind and whether we are conscious or not the flow of thoughts never stops. Most of us aren't aware of this constant flow, but it shapes who we are. Since thoughts precede action, it is our responsibility to observe our thoughts and make sure we don't fill it with negative self-talk.

What are negative thoughts? They are thoughts that we think unintentionally, innocent thoughts where negativity can hide. "I don't want this... I can't... I won't make it on my own..." on and on. There are so many examples, "I can't do this at my age... It's too difficult for me... I just can't." These thoughts disturb our reality and sabotage any potential we have.

So what can we do? We could replace the word "no" with "yes" and replace negative thoughts with positive ones. The question we must ask ourselves is "What do I want?" This is how I educated my daughters who were used to saying, "I **don't** want X." Then I asked my daughters, "So, what *do* you want?" They were then able to engage with what they wanted and with solutions to their problems.

Today, be aware of your thoughts. Pay attention to the negative ones sneaking in and ask yourself, "So, what *do* I want?"

April 9th

"Fake it until you make it."

Sometimes when we encounter obstacles or difficulties in life we tell ourselves, "If only I was braver, more energetic, more intelligent, more... more... more!" Character traits and behaviors are acquired through life and are then called experiences. Experienced sailors obtain their skills not by sailing the Pacific Ocean, but by dealing with storms. Similarly, we are also required to deal with new and scary challenges. After we have succeeded, we understand it was only fear that hindered us and was easier than we expected. Without meaning to, we've added another trait or skill to our tool box. The best way to overcome challenges is to not avoid them, because they will always pop up, but by simply faking the "missing" trait or skill by believing it's already in our toolbox. Faking a behavior ultimately makes it real.

Think about a challenge you have to face. It doesn't have to be world-changing, it may even be having that conversation you are avoiding. Think about what's preventing you from having that conversation and what you need to overcome it. An example could be needing bravery. You could just simply believe that you are already brave and then watch the miracles come.

Fake it until you make it.

April 10th

The fear of failure is often much stronger than the desire to succeed.
During our childhoods we, in a curious and natural way, explored many things. But then our parents sheltered us and warned us to not take risks. The educational system creates generations of disciplined students.

So life seems secure and comfortable even if that's not true. The fear of failure and the inability to take risks prevents us from reaching our potential and learning new things, which is important to our growth. Let's not give up opportunities because of fear of failure.

Your potential is waiting to be realized, give it the opportunity to express itself. Keep in mind that failure is the tuition that must be paid. It's okay, and you owe it to yourself to keep growing.

April 11th

There's a struggle in our mind between Good and Bad. That's our day-to-day reality. Both talk to us and advise us how to act in life and towards people. They often contradict each other. But, it's not about good or evil. We have the responsibility to choose. It's easy to run into the arms of avoidance and give up. But like everything in life, it has a price and profit.

Choosing the easy option (the bad) will make us annoy people or get angry at them. The price we pay is preventing ourselves from realizing our full potential. Choosing the good isn't easy and often requires effort, but growth and development doesn't exist without difficulty.

Today consciously choose the good.

April 12th

Remember that there is always someone listening to you, not *just* listening to you but taking your words very seriously. Your brain is constantly producing thoughts, the vast majority of them unaware that they are impacting the quality of life significantly. Often these automatic thoughts contain the seeds of suffering. When we're disappointed, frustrated or depressed the dam can sometimes break and we allow negative thoughts to sneak in and sabotage us. It could be a thought such as "I'm so stupid, I knew it wouldn't work, why even try, because I'm a loser" etc. Often these thoughts are the opposite of our reality, however what creates reality *is* our thoughts. Someone is listening to and analyzing your thoughts all the time and that's you. We must be aware of this and constantly work to convert negative thoughts into positive ones. And if we sometimes can't find the strength or the right words then simply say, "I love myself!" This will stop the negative thoughts from snowballing.

Today remind yourself that you love yourself! Say it passionately over and over again and feel the love flowing within you.

April 13th

One virtue we can embrace is keeping our composure.
There are many stressful situations in life. We seem to be accustomed to getting worked up about meaningless situations. We've gotten used to living dramatically. We've developed the habit of dividing everything into black or white, all or nothing. We've forgotten the other shades that really make up life. The media constantly depicts minor things as tragedies. It's presented by serious looking reporters who broadcast non-stop. Remaining calm will keep us in the present moment. Slow and controlled breathing and examining the situation will make it clear that there's panic for no reason.

Breathe and remember that everything is fine. Leave the drama to the movies.

April 14ᵗʰ

Who are you?

It's possible to write several volumes to this question, but I have chosen to focus on one unique aspect: truth. We have become accustomed to lying. Small, meaningless lies can be convenient for us, but as with everything, it slowly becomes second nature. Maybe it doesn't seem so terrible, but it hides our truth and takes away our responsibility for ourselves.

Coping with the truth and responsibility for ourselves are what defines us. Behind every little or big lie is fear; the fear of disappointment, consequences or coping with the circumstances! If we get into the habit of telling the truth with confidence our quality of life will improve. How do we do that? Slowly, and in moderation with awareness.

Be brave and take responsibility for your life. The results won't disappoint you.

April 15th

Failure is a matter of perspective.
In the worst cases we treat failure as a demon that is sabotaging our lives and success. This is the victim's mentality and it removes the responsibility we have for ourselves. It becomes a habit that paralyzes the spirit and creates an unwillingness to take the risks, ones we need to grow. The trap of staying in our comfort zone is that it may result in emotional discomfort and frustration. We allow ourselves to pretend to be happy when we are really not. That is the hidden cost, which is far greater than the cost of failure.

On the other hand, we could create a healthy relationship with failure. Its purpose is to teach us determination and to try again with a different approach. Only after failure do we learn to accept loss with grace. Nelson Mandela said, "There is no passion to be found playing small - in settling for a life that is less than the one you are capable of living."

Today, think about, "Forget the mistakes, remember the lessons." Face your past failures with gratitude and forgive yourself.

April 16th

You can choose to look at your life's events as random and without control of what's happening to you or you can choose to take responsibility for it by deciding how to react. Occasionally there'll be events or circumstances that seem to have the purpose of weakening you or cause you loss of control. But that's not really the intention, it's your interpretation. Life is like a swing, we go up and then down. We didn't invent it and we aren't the only ones experiencing it.

Accept what comes and get the most out of it. Remember that you learn and grow not from the easy victories, but from difficulties, effort and determination. Those are what shape your character. Sailors don't learn to sail in calm waters, the storms give them experience, maturity and the ability to confidently deal with the forces of nature.

Remember that the challenges are what make you grow!

April 17th

It's easy to concentrate on what we don't have.
This causes pain and a constant feeling of scarcity in money, sleep, leisure time, family time, etc. Most of us seem programmed to think this way. This isn't a healthy way of living life and in fact, sometimes reality is different. We tend to interpret it from the narrow monotonous gaze which we look at our lives with. However, there's an alternative, a much more sane and empowering way to look at life. See life as it exists. Why not look at what is already there and accept its existence? For example, quality time with family doesn't have to be measured in time but in the quality of listening, sharing, and loving.

April 18th

We have a constant monologue running in our heads.
Our stream of thoughts is infinite and unconscious. Conscious thought is just the tip of the iceberg. We can intervene with our stream of thoughts and plant empowering messages. These messages must be conscious and be planted proactively. For example, I planted the message, "Trust yourself, it will be alright." We must trust ourselves. Why trust others when we could trust ourselves?

Some of us have gotten used to relying on others to make decisions for us. Why trust others when we can trust ourselves? Get used to trusting yourself. The person who knows you the best is you and only you. Plant this empowering message in your mind. The conscious decisions you make will work the best for you. Train yourself to trust yourself. You won't be disappointed.

April 19th

If what I am telling you sometimes seems obvious it's because it is. I'm not here to say anything new, I'm only here to bring concepts into your awareness and consciousness. I want to show you what I see as the human condition and what we can do to change it. Let's begin with our physical bodies. The Western world diet is based on empty calories, processed snacks, sugar, food coloring and harmful chemicals. We're accustomed to eating and drinking these things. With all the time we spend on shopping and considering our food, it's not surprising that we drink little to no water. Fast food chains sell meals that come with soft drinks and other restaurant chains offer bottomless specials. The drinks that big corporations push on us damage our bodies over time and can cause diseases such as diabetes, tooth decay or obesity.

There's no doubt that it's hard to fight against endless advertising from Coca-Cola and Pepsi, but it's your right and responsibility to choose wisely about what to put into your body. Just as negative thoughts poison the mind, processed foods and drinks poison the body. Epidemics like diabetes, cancer and obesity didn't come out of nowhere, they were well cultivated. Simply take one small conscious step like choosing to drink one glass of water over a sugary drink. Doing that will add 365 glasses of water each year and subtract 365 sugary drinks from your diet.

I once read a book that discussed financial saving habits. The author explains that if we skip the coffee we buy on the way to work each morning, which is about $3, we'd save about $750 a year. Save your life like he saved his money. Bit by bit a massive change will begin.

April 20th

"Is it air that you breathe?" Morpheus asks Neo in the film *The Matrix*. It was not air. Everything was happening in Neo's subconscious; he was breathing dreams.

Consciousness creates reality, so one who is conscious is one who creates their reality. For example, phantom pregnancy is when the body experiences pregnancy symptoms, but is not pregnant. This can happen if someone believes that they are pregnant. Thoughts and desire translated into reality, making the body become what the mind wanted to see. This is why it's so important to only have positive thoughts. Persistence and clearly seeing the image of your desire is what will make dreams become reality.

Practice positive thinking. The amount you grow spiritually is limited by the size of your dreams. You owe it to yourself to try.

April 21th

Work with what you have.

Don't wait for an ideal situation. Sometimes we wait so long for the details to work out that we forget our original plan. It's normal to want many things, but we must act in order to achieve them. Don't wait for things to happen, it just prevents us from taking action, implementing our plans and achieving them. In most cases ideal conditions won't ever exist so we have to act with the tools we have available to us now.

We should continue to move forward even if it's by baby steps. These small movements will add up to become a large step and then a leap. A baby doesn't get up and start walking, it does so over time with determination and consistency. They fall, but they don't let the failures stop them. Have you ever heard an infant say, "Enough of this! I've fallen enough times. I'll never figure it out." There is no point waiting for an ideal situation because it will be too late once it happens, if it happens. We must realize that the only thing waiting does is stop us from acting and achieving. Worse is not trying at all.

So even if your circumstances are not ideal don't let that stop you. Just do it!

April 22th

Get used to thinking positively. Start from the moment you open your eyes in the morning.

No matter what your circumstances are, it's your interpretation of them that affects you. If you woke up to heavy rain and a headache and had an important presentation at work or a surgery that day press on. Everything passes, and though we can't stop time there's always more of it later. We must be aware of every moment and second and choose to think positive thoughts from the moment we wake up. Our first thought in the morning has a tremendous impact on our day. In the first moments of waking we transition from high-level consciousness to an earthly consciousness so it's extremely important to think positive thoughts.

Do it consciously so that negative thoughts don't sneak by in the morning mist.

April 23th

We sometimes tend to punish, be rigid, and criticize ourselves without good reason. Why be so strict and angry? Remember that we are human and everything is fine. Destructive criticism has no purpose other than to weaken us.

Are we really not good enough? And if so, in relation to whom and why? Are we measuring ourselves subjectively? Let's try to look at things from a broader perspective, a bird's eye view, where we can look at all factors. The more we know the more we can learn and the more we can forgive. This is a worthy substitute for destructive criticism.

April 24th

One of the most powerful tools that enables us to realize the infinite potential in us is the ability to take responsibility. Responsibility is one of the most important criteria for self-actualization since it makes us realize the smallness of our life. It's easy to blame others, circumstances or external factors for bad situations. It's the government, spouse, parents or employer that makes us feel so small. It's easy to blame others for creating the sad reality of our lives, whether it's truth or interpretation. Blaming others for our sins and lack of motivation allows us to feel justified in our failures. This is a mistake. Responsibility for our flaws brings us closer to perfection. It recognizes the value of self-importance. We must believe that we shape and create our lives and future with our thoughts. It's an empowering way to look at life and allows us to realize the potential within us.

It's time to take responsibility!

April 25th

Don't wait for someone else to take the first step. First, it may never happen. Second, it may be too late when it does and third, our ego is what drives us and your wants and needs may not be what their ego wants or needs. The weight rests on your own shoulders. Think about the precious moments you could have experienced if you had taken that first step. You don't have to feel that you are less if you fail, the opposite is true.

The moment you step off that cliff into the great unknown you grow and light up because you chose to initiate and take responsibility for your destiny. Good for you!

April 26th

I was told that to be successful I must be a lone wolf.

This is what guides my perspective. I don't need anyone, I can manage on my own. This probably had a profound effect on my career choice as an investment manager. There I could express my independence and make decisions myself. However, after a while I noticed the unhappiness that comes with living a solitary life. I became depressed, which probably stemmed from my ego protecting itself. I felt loneliness, detachment and displaced. Making money and winning cost me my soul.

The spiritual process I have gone through in recent years has led me to the conclusion that there are two main guiding forces. The first is fear, which disguises itself as anger, hatred or arrogance. The second is love, which expresses itself through courage, giving, optimism, forgiveness and empathy. Over time I began to recognize the power of a group. I realized that no one has monopoly over knowledge and that every one of us can create extraordinary results. We all carry an encyclopedia of life which are made from the experiences we've had during our time on earth. Power lies in asking for help from and co-operating with others. We must do it from a place of wanting to learn and grow. This approach challenges our ego, but the rewards are endless.

I invite you to observe the people around you at home, school, work, or wherever you are from a place of love and compassion. This perspective will make it easier for you to ask for help and allow you to understand the experiences of others. It's truly amazing.

April 27ᵗʰ

Where is happiness hiding?

Happiness is hiding in the present moment. Most of us aren't happy with what we're doing right now. We're doing one thing, but our hearts desire another. We're here, but we want to be elsewhere. We're in this century, but we would rather be in a different era. We're physically here, but our thoughts take us elsewhere. How can we compensate for this huge hole between what we have and what we want? Sometimes our solutions cause frustration and unhappiness as we try to change things that are too big for us to change alone.

Life is an interesting journey and the views are not always what we wished for. If we want to enjoy it, we must become a part *of* it and be present moment to moment, here *and* now.

Be here and now and see if you are happier. Pay attention to your thoughts since they have a tendency to wander. Be aware of when they do and gently shift your attention back to the here and now.

Today, take deep breaths. You will be present in this place, here *and* now.

April 28ᵗʰ

I start the morning with a thank you prayer where I congratulate myself for getting up and being ready for a new day.
I repeat that anything is possible and new beginnings are here before me. This prayer has the power to heal because it comes from a place of giving, the same kind of giving that a mother gives to her child and the innocent and unconditional love a baby gives its mother. According to the Torah, this is what supreme happiness is. It's the power of blessing. The sages also said that blessings bring good fortunes. Everyone who blesses is also blessed. Even when the energy that surrounds us is evil, let us count our blessings until our disappointment becomes hope or our concerns become peace. Wait for sadness to become joy and motivation for success.

We are blessed. Amen!

April 29th

My birthday.
When speaking about time I feel like I was born a minute ago and my passing will be in a blink of an eye. It's not a bad thing. It's my birthday today. I take advantage of this day to thank everyone who has brought me this far: God, my parents, my teachers, my acquaintances, my wife and, of course, myself. That's what's obvious. A birthday is a celebration for everybody. It reminds us of what we went through and where we are now. It also serves as a motivator for the future. Every passing year shows us how fleeting our lives are and we need to decide what our lives will look like and begin living it! Please don't get confused, fulfilling our lives isn't an easy task that provides instant gratification (which is an addictive drug that causes increased consumption and emotional debauchery). I'm talking about the fact that we have a spiritual entity, who is content with a little and doesn't require much to be happy. This entity seeks to develop and grow spiritually, and its reward is happiness. This kind of happiness is achieved by daily practice of accepting things as they are and internalizing that everything is okay. We haven't invented any new feelings; we won't ever feel something others haven't felt before. Humbly accept what there is, love it, and love yourself.
Have a happy birthday.

April 30ᵗʰ

I assume you've heard the saying, "A journey of a thousand miles begins with a single step."
This is true with everything in life. You don't have to conquer Everest, but you do have to fulfill your dreams. The goal seems so far away sometimes and maybe even impossible to reach. Maybe it will only be partially fulfilled or maybe it will take you longer than others do, but it's still something that needs to be done!

Start with a single step. Most people don't even try to take the first step. Get on the path and walk on it. A wise saying is "Aim for the moon. If you miss, you may hit a star."

Start today with one small step towards the goal you dared to dream about, but haven't yet fulfilled.

Go!

May

May 1ˢᵗ

Sometimes you'll feel lonely even if you're surrounded by family and friends.
Suddenly, you'll feel lonely, empty and helpless. Existential loneliness is normal and part of being human. However, you have a powerful tool: spirituality. It's available to you at all times! When you feel loneliness take over, turn to your spiritual side that is connected with everything. Seek to be filled with infinite and comforting compassion. Talk to the higher power that guides and accompanies you; it will be happy to listen to you and give you a sense of belonging. Intuitively, you should know that you are not alone. There is always someone watching over and looking out for you. You are not alone, even in the most difficult moments of your life when it feels like you are.

May 2nd

Sometimes we feel like we didn't wake up on the right side of our comfy queen sized bed.

We're only human and because of that we'll experience failure, mood changes, depression and frustration. It's an integral part of life, not a bad thing. It simply is. However, there is something to do about it. Our imagination is a powerful tool and our mind can only contain one thought at a time, so there are many ways to alleviate our negative feelings. At the beginning it can be a bit difficult, but over time, determination and perseverance will make the process easier.

You can listen to your favorite music or watch an exciting and cathartic movie. You can go out for a run or just do something fun. Try sharing your happy feelings with your loved ones, they always know how to inspire you. Notice how your feelings improve. Remember that you're a miracle even though it's not always obvious. All the obstacles and difficulties are a part of life!

Be aware of your thoughts and if you don't have anything kind to whisper to yourself keep quiet or look at yourself in the mirror and remember... you love yourself!

May 3rd

Like an unrestrained dictator it attacks with all of its strength,
using its nuclear weapons with no discretion. It will create distractions with no hesitation when someone tries to harm it. It is neither good nor bad, it's a tool, a powerful tool. It's our job to tame it and train it, otherwise it will run wild. Get to know the ego. The bodyguard of honor. Attack first and check later, it performs its job with enviable credibility, but it leaves destruction behind. We've more or less learned to get along with it, but we must know it in depth to understand that in its good way it causes the bad! Many wars are based on ego. Lost dignity on a national level paired with the desire to humiliate those who had humiliated them. But now that a line has been crossed, do we say that's enough?

It's up to us. The ego is one of our management tools, it defends our honor and makes sure that we won't feel humiliated. The battle plan of the ego is to weaken its competition then go in for the kill. It isn't growth, it's a survival based strategy useful only in survival. But, we are beyond that. We've discovered that we can be fulfilled with our lives, with life itself and spiritual growth. We have the responsibility to restrain our ego and reduce its dominance in our lives so that we can have a fruitful relationship with others; our partners, friends, family, acquaintances and the multitude of people that we come in contact with throughout our lives. It doesn't mean that we have to give anything up, the voice of common sense is our peaceful companion that is with us, it's truth is said quietly, sometimes in a whisper. Listen to it as well, it has wisdom to share.

Practice restraining the ego, listen to your inner voice and try to find the road of compromise. Practice compromise with your family, acquaintances, and see if things turn out more harmoniously.

May 4th

Start your morning with a light conversation with the person you love the most. Remind yourself why you love you and if you can't think of anything forgive yourself for your failings. You are only human, just a small part of the miracle of creation. So, before you jump out of bed for the day, lay for another minute with your eyes closed. Savor the tranquility and imagine yourself starting the day happy and joyful. Then go!

Good morning!

May 5th

I remember this amazing Xbox ad as a child. A woman was giving birth and put in so much effort that the baby went flying into the clouds. While it's flying the baby's body and voice changes as it goes through the cycle of life. By the time of its descent it was old and had rotten teeth. The journey ends when it suddenly lands in it's tombstone. The commercial then says, "Life is short, play more." It's an ingenious advertisement that shows us our entire life in a few seconds.

The pace of modern life is accelerated. Life is short and death is only a matter of time. When you reach old age you start looking back with regret. So, from now on make every minute count.

Imagine yourself when you're old. Think about how you would like your life to be and work toward that vision now! Remember life is short. Live it!

May 6th

Be your own gardener.
There's nothing more endearing than a manicured garden with flowers bursting from freshly turned soil surrounded by trimmed and healthy green grass. This magnificent garden didn't sprout by itself. Before the beauty there was extensive planning, investment and continuous upkeep that included weeding and work to maintain healthy green grass and vibrant colorful flowers. Like a garden, such is our mind.

Often, like neglected gardens or the wild, thorns grow and climb our mind and darken our thoughts and life. We the gardeners, whether we like it or not, must constantly work to create a healthy garden. We must weed out negative thoughts, trim the fears, sweep the frustration and plant beds of calmness. We need to plant flowers for peace, seeds of hope, sprouts of compassion, and water it all with happiness. We will see how the garden slowly changes as it blossoms and blooms. This garden will accompany us our whole life and if we decide to take time off or give up no one will be there to replace us.

Without constant attention your mental garden will lose its way. We must be vigilant at all times, not out of necessity, but out of choice. Choose to cultivate and grow your garden in a healthy and joyous way because it's the right thing to do for yourself. Life is growth and we can have a big part in it. So, let's plant with joy.

Take a few minutes today to work on your mental garden. Dig up a small spot that is filled with wild unattended thoughts and plant positive ones instead. Cultivate your garden slowly, consciously and with attention to detail.

May 7th

Pull the strings yourself.

Who controls you? Is it your partner, your kids, your parents, your boss, your friends? Maybe that's where the anger that radiates out of you comes from. Are you being controlled and manipulated to behave in a certain way? The only way is with your cooperation. You allow these things to happen out of the need to please and make sure that others will continue liking you.

But do we really have control over what others think of us? Is it really our business what others think of us? One of the best things we can do is cherish ourselves for who we are. Understand that what others think about us is their right, but that shouldn't stop us from being ourselves. We're the miracle of creation, a miracle that must be nurtured. So let's do that for ourselves.

Be aware of the subconscious attempts of others to control and manipulate you.

Choose freedom!

May 8th

You deserve it!

You *do* deserve it and there's no one more suitable for it than you. In many areas of our lives great things happen even when we have nothing to do with it. And I want to say: You deserve it.

This concept became clear to me when a coworker asked me for a ride home. Of course, I was happy to take him home. I wanted to drive him to the entrance of his building, but he insisted that I let him off on the main road so I wouldn't have to go right into his neighborhood. He said he could walk from there. I told him he didn't need to bother, I would take him all the way. Despite my insistence he insisted more. He already felt like I was doing him a big favor that he didn't deserve! I remembered a lecture given by Arnold Schwarzenegger at a graduation ceremony where he detailed his perception of life. He said "I take what I can get." This is what we're talking about, getting the things you have worked and worried about. There's no need to point out who will fulfill their life goals. Life is too short for us to procrastinate or to believe that anyone is superior to us or that we don't deserve infinite abundance just like anyone else.

Take the abundance and overcome the shyness, fear and need to justify yourself. Simply take a piece of the pie because you deserve it!

May 9th

Sometimes we go through dark periods in our life. It seems like everything we do brings us negative results and that there's no hope- just utter despair. It's horrible to feel despair, a lack of belonging and unhappiness. But it happens to everybody, it's a part of the human experience. The clouds eventually disappear over time (even though of course we'd be happy to get rid of it immediately).

So, what can you do? This is where the distinction between two key insights becomes important. One option is to try and control things and the second is to take responsibility. Control is an illusion since we can't really control circumstances. All we can do is accept the situation and take responsibility for our actions. Everything passes and often time is the best medicine. Therefore, instead of fighting and resisting simply strive to accept the circumstances and take responsibility for your feelings and behaviors. Understand that this is a part of everyone's life. Winston Churchill put it well when he said, "If you're in hell keep going." And I'm adding "Until you reach the exit sign."

Don't lose hope if you're experiencing a difficult time. Keep going through it. The exit sign is waiting for you.

May 10th

Listen to the God within you.

Intuition is the way the divine guides you. The background noise surrounds us and our thoughts distract us from our intuition and knowledge of what is right for us. Very often we feel our intuition, but we aren't listening to it because we are worried by logic, inner chatter, or others' advice. So, what is the right way to reach this divine intuition that guides us in its calm way through the stormy sea? Well, the "devil" speaks to us by yelling and God talks to us by "whispering".

Today listen to the small whispers which conveys God's messages to us.

May 11th

Everyone sets their own limits, but if we broke through our limitations then everyone would be able to succeed. It sounds logical and most of us probably already follow these rules. But who determines our limitations? Is it you? Probably not, you're just listening to someone who judged you based on their own experiences or out of fear that you'll succeed and leave them behind in the dark.

What are your limitations? What are your abilities? You think you have a clue but you are probably wrong. Our limitations are imaginary lines that we draw for ourselves. The reality TV show *Survival* demonstrates this. The show presents models who eat insects whole, skinny people who lift heavy loads and average people like us who dive into icy water for longer than they thought possible all in order to avoid elimination. This program shows us how people cross their imaginary line, something that doesn't seem possible in everyday life.

What lines have you drawn for yourself? Isn't it time to cross it and leave it behind in the dust?

May 12th

What do you need to be a better version of yourself?
Not much actually, just a plan and small but aware and determined steps towards it. A daily walk on the path of growth will make you better tomorrow than you are today. The change is imperceptibly slow, but keep walking this path and over time it will bring you to new heights of consciousness where you can experience the true meaning of being human and a miracle of life. You don't have to invest much. Start by always doing the best you can regardless of the circumstances, over time your judgments will slowly disappear.

Regrets will also vanish because all you have ever done is the best you could!

May 13th

The fastest way to go crazy is to look for logic in this illogical world.
Logic is completely subjective. When we are in an irrational situation frustration bubbles up within us. After all, "it doesn't make sense." We say this to ourselves over and over again while our frustration keeps rising, draining us of energy and leaving us weak.

"It doesn't make sense" that this candidate won, "it doesn't make sense" how much this cost, "it doesn't make sense" that you have to stand in line for two hours. What doesn't make sense is our attitude about these situations. It's a sure way to go crazy. Stop looking for logic, it's subjective. Our planet is so great and varied that everywhere you go there will be different laws, regulations, and customs.

When you encounter irrational situations, accept them and smile. I'm not saying you should give up. It's okay and even desirable to convert frustration, anger and injustice to growth and change. Energy that flows out of you from pure desire creates a better reality.

To do this, calmly accept reality without judging it. Then, ask yourself how you can create a better reality and just do it. You won't always succeed, but try and fail, don't fail to try.

May 14th

How do you listen?

Do you already know what someone wants to say? Have you formulated an opinion before they finished talking? It's common to listen with one ear and with an opinion. This is automatic listening, where we're prepared with responses that don't empower or improve the situation of others. but just closes the door on the conversation. How many times has it happened to you? And what was the result? Did it help the other side? Did it instill hope or a solution? Or did it end with the other side feeling frustrated? I know it's hard to listen sometimes, but it's the true meaning of a healthy and constructive interaction. Listen as you would expect others to listen to you. Take in their words, make eye contact and listen to what is really bothering them. People want to be listened to, understood, and accepted.

Give them what they want! Pay full attention, it makes a difference!

May 15th

Interact with yourself positively.

Do you want to be around a grumbling, upset person who is hard to please, or a smiling, patient one who listens and tries to help?

Which one are you? Spiritual growth cannot occur without positive thinking, optimism and self-commitment towards growth. When you grow spiritually people will seek your advice and company. Become someone who is easy to please.

Take responsibility for your life because it will allow you to understand the many faces of human beings. Everyone has different needs and wants. It's not our job to judge others or criticize their actions. The variety of opinions, choices and possibilities that exist for each and every one of us is what sets us apart. We only have to accept each other, even when we don't understand each other. How easy life is when we learn to respect the other's choices.

Why not choose to turn every interaction into something positive? Strive to empower every person you meet and see how empowerment will come right back to you.

May 16th

Responsibility.

It's so important for spiritual growth because without it the experiences that we encounter can cause us to become victims. Failure to take responsibility is like handing over the keys of our life to someone else. We will not evolve or grow. It may be convenient to a certain extent, but if we are trying to better ourselves then not taking responsibility will eventually frustrate us as we won't be where we want to be. We must utilize our freedom of choice. We are choosing every moment and if we are not it's because we have chosen not to choose. Once we take responsibility for our thoughts, feelings and reactions we become masters of ourselves. We won't need to look for victims to blame, become paralyzed with fear or allow the circumstances to shake us.

If we want to change our situation we just have to take responsibility and choose differently!

May 17th

Life is an endless race. At least that's how the Western world feels.

We have infinite tasks, bills and responsibilities. We must finish everything quickly or else others will be angry with us, disappointed in us, or we get fined. We're trapped like hamsters in a running wheel; we don't get anywhere. Our tasks are repetitive or are rigidly scheduled. Do we really need to take on so much? A side effect is reduced sleep. We sleep much less than our parents or grandparents slept. There are also those who treat sleep as a waste of time.

We'll never get everything done and the tasks will just pile up. It's up to us. We can choose the amount of tasks we want to do each day. Let's get rid of the addiction to work and just be in the present moment. Let's slow down and carefully choose the tasks we want to do. Let's have more time for ourselves so when peace comes we are present for it and our inner voice can come alive.

Slow down and breathe. Everything's fine!

May 18th

The process of spiritual growth requires constant learning.
Curiosity and desire for exploration is something we naturally have as kids. It also exists in us as adults, but we forget about it. We must allow curiosity and exploration back into our lives so we can continue to learn and grow.

It will also allow those around us to grow, even if at a slower pace. To grow we must always strive to do the right thing, create enthusiasm for life and encourage others and ourselves to constantly learn new things.

The world is big and knowledge is infinite so let's make the most out of it and enjoy it. Have a lovely day.

May 19th

Excuses, excuses, excuses.
Some of us have a PHD in it. There's no point in them. They prevent us from dealing with the problem, learning from it, and from standing on our own and making sure our presence is powerful. Excuses weaken us and make us blame everyone else for the situation. Excuses allow us to procrastinate. Is that what you want? Overcome excuses by taking a stand and by taking responsibility. It's difficult, scary and requires us to navigate situations ourselves, but when we take that initiative we end up with many choices available to us.

When you're responsible you're not paralyzed by fear, you feel powerful and alive! You trust yourself and don't need to blame others, feel fear or lose control. Take responsibility now! No excuses.

May 20th

Focus on the little things.
That is my goal for you today. We get up in the morning, finish our chores hurriedly, brush our teeth on autopilot, and say goodbye. Is that us? Or is it another part of us? Most of the time we aren't mentally there. Thoughts wander far, but these are the little things that make up life. So why not focus on them and put ourselves in the present moment?

Remember that all we have is this moment. Let's focus on it. The past is gone and the future is still out there. Everything we have is here now. Let's take a deep breath and slowly lift our head up and look around us. What do we see? We see life as it is. Let's focus on the little things and give them the attention they deserve. Our life is made up of tiny units of time and we should be present in every unit. Let's really be there. Let's focus on the now. Breathe, observe and listen.

Have a lovely day.

May 21th

Which reality do we choose to see?
More than 15 years ago, an impression that I'll never forget was engraved in my heart. One ordinary morning, the woman who later became my wife, got ready to go to work. What she didn't know was that in a few hours we would land in Crete for a long weekend vacation. Her surprise and excitement when the plan was revealed were great. In the evening, as we sat at the hotel restaurant, we heard a conversation between another couple. The husband was complaining about the hotel and room to his wife. It seemed that this wasn't the vacation they were expecting, the hotel and the room didn't meet their expectations at all. After a few minutes they finished eating and headed off. As I looked away I spotted another, yet slightly older, couple. The man was smiling. I asked him how his vacation was going and he said "it's so wonderful, the view is breathtaking, the hotel is amazing and the room is luxurious." Wow, the same situation, but with two different perspectives. I dare say that their points of view were as different as day and night. These conversations left a strong impression on me.

Reality was the same for all of us, so what was different? The expectations! One couple had high expectations which were hard to satisfy and the other chose to enjoy what they had. It's all a matter of choice, conscious choice!

You can consciously choose to be content and, as I end with other insights, everything is fine.

May 22th

To one degree or another we all have the tendency to avoid things that frighten us.
In our imagination thoughts of failure and terrible consequences run wild. Ultimately, the worst thing to do is allow fear to keep us from action. We miss opportunities in our lives due to avoidance.

Be brave and walk with fear. Pursue your dreams, it's solely in your hands. Whatever you do now won't interest anyone in one hundred years anyways. Live in the moment! True, sometimes you'll fail, but growth and learning come from failure. Most importantly, don't fail to try.

May 23th

Do circumstances determine our fate?

Will a low starting point prevent us from realizing our potential? There's no shortage of examples of people who have reached greatness when starting from nothing. Google, Apple, Microsoft and Facebook were all created by ordinary people who were brave enough to chase their vision. These are people whose starting point wasn't different from others in the Western world. By the way, there's no shortage of these examples in other parts of the world too. What unites them is that they didn't let their circumstances determine what they could do. They didn't succumb to thoughts like "I'm not rich enough." "No one knows who I am." "I don't have the tools or knowledge to get started." What they did do was focus on their next steps until they got to the next level and gained more experience. Their belief in their abilities pushed them forward. These people realized their personal potential. We should do the same and focus on our growth to become the best version of ourselves.

Make this your way of life. You will experience an increase in happiness, energy, optimism, joy and trust in yourself, regardless of the circumstances.

May 24th

We have something that never rests.

I'm not talking about our hearts or breathing, I'm talking about the highway of thoughts that run non-stop. This stream of thoughts is mostly unconscious, but we can control our mind and choose what's allowed on the highway. We must make a habit of observing thoughts as a bystander without judgment. What are my thoughts? Do they contain hope, compassion, and love or fear, apprehension, worry and despair? It's usually not black and white, thoughts of love can coexist with thoughts of fear.

Your thoughts belong to you and you can learn to filter them. Put tolls on your highways where entry is only allowed for constructive, powerful or positive thoughts. There are a lot of wild thoughts so sometimes there will be slipups. It's okay, don't try to fight them, just replace those thoughts with more powerful ones. It seems difficult or even impossible, but daily practice will lead to improvement and the effort will pay off as positive thoughts create a positive life. You will achieve feelings of peace, tranquility and hope. Negative thoughts only create fear, doubt and anxiety.

So, what are you going to choose?

May 25th

The quiet acceptance of life is essential to understanding enlightenment.
Enlightenment is a true and sincere acceptance of the here and now. It's an understanding that this is all there is, this moment, and that everything is fine. It's not good or bad, there's no judgment or criticism, there is only this moment. It's refusing to surrender to the ordinary sense of the word. It's not passive behavior, it's a peaceful acceptance of what is.

Enlightenment is inner peace and excitement about the miracle of life. Enlightenment provides renewal of energy, freshness and satisfaction!

May 26th

What are you giving up today?
Is it a conversation with your boss about a higher salary? Is it a scary, yet important conversation with your kids? Are you constantly living by giving up? Do you prefer to keep sleeping and not deal with things?

We all fear something, but the actions we take are what make us different. Once we decide to give up something that is important to us, we run the risk of feeling like we're missing out. We must remember that even if we tried something scary and the results weren't as we hoped, we still experienced growth and broke boundaries. Loss is momentary, but concession and the feeling of missing out is permanent!

Don't give up on things that are important to you and especially, don't give up on yourself.

May 27th

You may have seen or heard about movies where the main character is told they have several hours or days left to live. In the film we see how the main character behaves with this information. They're cold and alienated, they have trouble feeling satisfaction, they are disconnected with their parents, spouse or children. When there's no time left, the protagonist forms a new relationship with themselves and their environment. They are trying to mend the broken relationships and trying to bring out their compassion, kindness, listening skills and acceptance.

Do we have to wait for these moments in order to be better to ourselves and those around us? We must learn to look at people and things with curiosity, enthusiasm and like it's the last time we will see them. This will allow us to act with compassion and love. Believe me, I speak from personal experience, the things you can accomplish will look like miracles. We have to learn to cherish and praise what's around us and to be grateful for our life. The result is inevitably happiness.

Do it now; look around you, look up at the sky in awe. Everything is fine and the drama is small and unimportant when you are learning to grow.

May 28th

Multitasking.
A commonly used term in Information Technology. An operating system has the ability to run multiple applications at the same time. As long as you get enough computing power and have enough memory, you can do almost anything. Our brain is different. Thoughts move in a one-lane road so we can't add other thoughts, we can only replace the existing one.

Humans are not built for multitasking. Thoughts can only happen one at a time and they create our inner world, our emotions, our actions and finally, our reality. This process of creating your own reality happens in serial order and it's the least stressful way to operate.

In this modern world with instant solutions and quick answers multitasking has become popular. Tasks can get done simultaneously. But, multitasking comes with a heavy price tag. First, there's a great deal of shallowness, superficiality and mediocre results. The quality of our products is poor when compared to products that require dedication. What's more is that our feeling of satisfaction isn't as great. We just feel exhausted and empty. Eventually, we will collapse and have nervous breakdowns, chronic fatigue, migraines, mental illnesses or depression.

Leave multitasking to computers and concentrate on one thing at a time in a deep, focused and intentional way. You'll feel more satisfied, more connected to yourself and you'll actually produce more. It's important to consider, where do all these endless tasks come from? Do you really need them? Can some be given up or handed over?

May 29th

Be your own gatekeeper.
Are you willing to let anyone into your home and without invitation? Does it make sense to let others come in with muddy shoes and walk around your house? Of course not. What you aren't willing to do in your home, you must not do in your mind. You've probably heard things people said to weaken you. Have you let this destructive thought enter your mind and damage it? Did it happen when your boss drew attention to your failures or when your parents who wanted you to be a certain way stopped you from trying things on your own?

Just as you guard your doorstep and decide who enters your home, do the same with your mind. Stand in the doorway and consciously decide to only allow thoughts that benefit and empower you to come in. Dirty thoughts like dirty shoes, they are welcome to stay elsewhere.

Become your mind's gatekeeper now!

May 30th

I remember reading an interview about a private detective who was hired by people to spy on family members, employees, friends or others. He said that what he was looking for was a change in someone's routine. We too have our own routines, about 90% of our actions are repeated daily. We are just recreating yesterday, and yesterday was recreated from the day before, etc. We are quite predictable.

If we are unsatisfied then we need to change our routine. I recommend making changes and forming new habits slowly. A drastic and radical change can stress us out and we will fall back into old habits. Significant change happens over time and begins with small steps. For example, weight loss can happen quickly, but eventually one goes back to their old eating habits and the weight is gained back. "Slow and steady wins the race" has always been a powerful adage.

When I decided to switch to a healthier diet I started in a gradual manner. First, I gave up soft drinks and switched to water. After only a couple of weeks I saw how much better I felt, without all that sugar and other chemicals my heartburn decreased. Then, I moved onto the next step and I reduced my meat intake from once a day to three times a week. Step by step I changed my diet significantly, but since it was done gradually the changes were almost painless and my new habits seamlessly replaced the old harmful ones. Weight loss came naturally and I felt energized. I've continued to make diet changes, such as cutting out simple carbs, dairy products and simple sugars, but all gradually. I've replaced unhealthy foods with healthy foods like whole carbs, soy milk, tofu, legumes and complex sugars such as fruit, honey, stevia, etc.

Start now! Think about a habit that you would be happy to get rid of and what you would like to replace it with. Just do it.

May 31ᵗʰ

Successful people focus most of their attention on what they want. They ask themselves "What do I want?" and "What can I do to get it?" There's always the question of "What can I do to move myself forward?"

The dietary changes that I've made in recent years have given me energy, vitality, lightness, and weight loss. I say no to simple carbohydrates, dairy and simple sugars. I've noticed that a significant portion of the western diet is based on these three foods. Every time I'm shopping or watching TV I'm met with a bombardment of products with the best packaging and advertising. The pictures are tempting and the packaging is colorful, but the nutrition is poor and harmful over time. Therefore, I am conscious to not go near most of the food products in stores or near most of the dishes offered in restaurants. Today there are so many nutritious and delicious food substitutes, and most of my diet consists of nuts, seeds, fruits, vegetables, legumes, whole grains, complex carbohydrates, milk substitutes and complex sugars.

Try to change your diet, you'll feel better!

June

June 1ˢᵗ

The wealthiest person is the one who is happiest with what he already has.

This powerful statement reflects what we should strive for. How many of us really cherish and appreciate what we have right now? We live in a time of abundance that allows for limitless money and consumption of material goods that we often cannot afford. If we stopped for a moment and looked around, it would be apparent that we have more than enough to make ourselves happy. It's okay to strive for more, but the question is what is the price we pay? If we could restrain ourselves and consume less and save more, I'm sure we'd all be happier in the long run. The biggest problem humans have is restraining ourselves. We lose control and honor our impulses, not our logic. We're conditioned to a life of obsession over the search for happiness that can't be achieved because as soon as we find some happiness we'll be searching for more.

June 2nd

Let's stop acting like circus elephants.

There's a legend about an elephant who, from the moment it was born, was meant to be in the circus. As a baby it didn't have too much power. It was tied to a wooden pole and couldn't free itself even though it tried many times. Over time the elephant grew and became stronger and though it was still tied to the same weak pole, it couldn't free itself. It wasn't the lack of physical strength that prevented it from running free, but the ingrained belief that it could never free itself from the wooden pole. If the elephant only tried to free itself now it could see how easy it was.

So why are we stuck? Since childhood we've been tied to several wooden poles of our own that we can't break free from. These could be beliefs about ourselves, our abilities or our actions. However, our childhood views should have no meaning today. Let's stop for a moment and think about what is blocking us from growing. What poles are we tied to? Poles that are easy to be free of if we only try?

Think what wooden poles you're attached to and start freeing yourself of them one by one. You'll see how easy it is.

June 3rd

When we look back at our hesitations, doubts, fears and anxieties they seem so meaningless. However, at the time all of our private emotions were hung out for the entire world to see. Quitting a job is followed by the anxiety of how to live, how to pay for expenses, or the decision to separate from your partner, etc. At that moment the sky seems to have fallen, but in hindsight it was a small hindrance. The devil, in the end, wasn't as terrible as he had seemed in the beginning. The paralysis and anxiety in those first moments quickly dissipated, but it had felt like a lifetime.

Most people end up not regretting things they did, but things that they didn't do. This is life, the path is uncertain and comfort is an illusion that doesn't allow us to grow from our failures. A butterfly doesn't learn how to immediately fly, it struggles at first to get up. It struggles against gravity and wind and eventually becomes strong enough to keep itself up. Like the butterfly we can also learn how to fly.

Find a challenge that keeps you feeling alive and perform this simple exercise every day. Imagine yourself in a decade: Where are you? What were you afraid of? Think about it. Imagine it and feel the fear dissipate as it's replaced by enthusiasm and hope.

June 4th

The trick is to get up one more time...

Everything that we experience in our lives is ours and ours alone. The opening of the Book of Ecclesiastes said, "There's nothing new under the sun." This universal truth was developed thousands of years ago. Tens of thousands of people have experienced successes and failures. There are sad moments and happy moments, crises and successes. There are moments where we fall and moments where we climb. This is life, a kind of roller coaster. You can't avoid this ride just like you can't avoid death. The right thing for us to do is to understand the rules in the game that have existed since the creation of man. Opposing these rules is useless and will just create suffering and unhappiness. We must accept that we'll lose relatives and friends, we'll experience difficulties, failures, disappointments, broken hearts, etc. It's something that life gives us and as much as we want to avoid it, we can't.

The trick is simply to get up one more time, just one more time, and shake off the dust and continue on. It's not always easy and when we're in turmoil it can sometimes seem impossible, but any other choice is unbearable and contrary to the miracle of life. We experience this life only once, and our perception and understanding of our rules is what will determine our direction of growth. Therefore, in order to continue growing and advancing in life we have to get up one more time.

Today, as you get ready to start your day, know that there will be failures, obstacles, rejections and disappointments. It's part of the game and you'll fall along the way, but get up one more time, only once more.

June 5th

Why did you get up this morning?
I'm not talking about why you physically got up. I'm not talking about the responsibilities or tasks that you need to do. I'm talking about the excitement, the love of life that wakes you up. There are people who wake up only because they didn't die the night before. Many people feel like that, but it's not a healthy way to start the day, nor is it a way to live happily.

As children we didn't like going to bed because we felt like we were missing out on life while we slept. In the mornings we woke up happy and ready to start the new day. Slowly, the difficulties of becoming an adult started to creep in and tire us to the point of exhaustion. Endless tasks assault us... material constraints, chores and workplace demands cause many of us to reach a state of desperation and lack of vitality as we become slaves to debt and society. This may be a paradigm, however, it doesn't *have* to be this way. Your reality can change, but only when your attitude does. If you can accept the thoughts and beliefs your mind has then you will have the power to change it.

If you want things to be different, change your thoughts and approach until *you* become different. Start practicing now. Help yourself by realizing that everything is okay even when it doesn't seem like it. Act with the knowledge that you have the power to change your life and your degree of happiness. Find your motivation, explore your dreams and desires and act on them. With perseverance and determination you will slowly become a better you.

June 6th

We often stand frozen when we have difficulty making a choice. We might turn to our relatives and ask them what the right decision is. Some of us choose to leave our decisions in the hands of others. Why is it so difficult to make a decision for ourselves? What's behind our painful indecision? The answer is **fear**.

Being afraid of making mistakes is what paralyzes us. Fear takes advantage, jumps to the front of the stage and tries to run the show! In these situations we're paralyzed, frozen and unable to make a choice. It isn't the mistake that scares us, but the fear of *making* the mistake that ultimately frightens us. As a human being one of the most effective ways to learn is by trying, failing and trying again. Allowing the paralysis of indecision to overwhelm us causes us to sit by idly and takes away our input on our lives.

Life is about growth and part of the process is making mistakes. The biggest lesson to be learned is don't repeat the same mistake twice. Simply learn from the mistake and move on. Our fear will be there on our journey. We have the responsibility to learn how to use it so it will protect us, but not limit us. We must continue to try and fail so that we may learn about ourselves. And we must never fail to try.

Think about this today while you're debating about a choice you need to make. What are the feelings behind your decision and is the fear something you can use or is it using you?

Make a decision even if you *know* it could be a mistake. It's okay, we're only human.

How else are we to learn?

June 7th

Be optimistic!
There are those who adopt this approach and live by it. It's all a matter of choice. If you have to choose, why not choose to be optimistic? It's clear that thought precedes perception of reality. The choice of optimism is a conscious choice born out of joy and gratitude for life. There are many reasons to be optimistic, if we can only realize them. Pessimism is a slippery slope that leads to apathy, bitterness and a lack of vitality. Is that what we really deserve? Is this the life we imagined when we were children, laughing at everything? Definitely not.

Be optimistic. Sometimes things don't turn out the way we planned and unfortunate situations can arise, but we can choose how to react. So, let's choose to be optimistic. Eventually thoughts will become actions so if we give ourselves the ability to be optimistic in every situation we can only benefit.

Optimism has many virtues such as joy, happiness, calmness, serenity, and the sense that everything is okay even in the most difficult situations. Optimism assures us that rejuvenation is coming.

Remember the saying, "It's better to be optimistic and wrong than pessimistic and right!"

June 8th

Don't become the problem.

Many times we get into situations where we feel like we are losing control. It could be an argument with your partner in which we say things that we later regret. It could also be an argument with your boss or with a stranger while standing in line. An innocent phone call with a customer representative or vice versa, can become heated and personal. In retrospect, we always regret our poor reaction and often don't understand how such poison came out of our mouths.

These reactions happen because sometimes we simply have automatic responses that do not take our values into account. In fact, being reactive cancels out our true character and we become puppets dancing to the words of others. To develop resilience we must cling to our truth, even when everything seems incomprehensible and set against us.

Keeping calm and taking responsibility isn't a simple thing, but it's a behavior that is developed over time. Be yourself, think of what you want to say and how you want to say it. Act with determination, but calm determination.

Change happens when you cling to the truth and don't react irrationally. Your power creates calmness and sends out a message to the universe that you are in control of your thoughts and behavior. You are not going to cooperate with any forms of manipulation. Not reacting badly or thoughtlessly allows you to be your true best self!

Start now!

June 9th

Think of your potential, it's the best version of you. Your potential is real, significant, and it's not being utilized. Your potential is your model, it's the upgraded version of you. Your potential is smart, energetic and has high self-esteem. Your potential knows how to say the right thing in every situation. You have charisma, self-discipline, determination and optimism. In fact, it's just the You that hasn't been revealed yet. The potential within you is similar to the block of marble that Michelangelo carved David out of. Michelangelo believed that the perfect sculpture was already inside the marble. He realized the beauty imprisoned within. Similarly, your potential is already in you. You just need to discover it and carve it out.

Think of the upgraded version of you already existing within your core. Imagine it slowly rising within you and leading your life.

June 10th

From a young age we are encouraged to succeed and specialize. We are told to work hard so that we can achieve a kind of success that will feel like heaven. However, for many people, by the time they get to heaven they're exhausted from the effort.

Excellence on paper is a sublime thing. Many successful people had to strive for success: basketball players, Olympic athletes, singers, etc. There is nothing wrong with taking your gift and turning it into the driving force of your life. Many of us strive for excellence in fields we aren't meant for and therefore pay the price of happiness. How many workaholics do you know who are truly happy with their lives? The need to strive for excellence is embedded in us from the time we're born.

The consequence is paralysis in other areas of our lives where we don't feel like champions. How many times have you said to yourself "I don't know how to dance" or "I don't know how to play basketball" or "I'm not a good runner"? Even though you want to do all of those things you avoid them because you aren't as skilled as you'd like to be. I suggest you treat excellence as a general principle and strive to achieve it in all the areas of your life you are enthusiastic about. Take the motivation and use it as the center of everything you do. Don't let obtaining success sabotage your family, your happiness, your leisure time or your attitude towards yourself.

Learn to accept mediocrity in your life so you don't have to suffer the unavoidable consequence of exhaustion. You should always give yourself the freedom to participate in all of life's experiences even if you don't excel at it.

June 11ᵗʰ

"Surely the fate of human beings is like that of the animals; the same fate awaits them both. As one dies, so dies the other. All have the same breath; humans have no advantage over animals. Everything is meaningless. All go to the same place; all come from dust, and to dust all return." (Ecclesiastes 3:19)

Most of you have probably heard of the fight or flight response. Animals have these responses as well, but humans are the only animals with consciousness. It's necessary for humans to survive in nature. It's automatic and sparks into action as soon as we feel like we're in danger. In this period of time, however, it's rarely triggered by real danger. Sometimes we're triggered by insults, anger, frustration, jealousy, surprise, etc. The fight or flight mechanism causes immediate alertness that can manifest in anxiety or attack. For example, it can happen in arguments between two people in a relationship where tensions are high and the disagreement can elicit their survival responses which goes far beyond what is necessary. After some time they can admit that things have gone too far and they investigate why. Somewhere between the flight or fight response and our automatic responses we can distinguish ourselves from the rest of the animals and choose how we want to react!

We can neutralize our flight or fight responses, but you must still recognize that it happens automatically and not necessarily because we have chosen this behavior. We can still bring about great change and neutralize our automatic responses. We can choose to listen and be vulnerable. It's how healing and growth begin.

Make choices that set you apart from the rest of the animals. Bring out your human qualities as this is where your growth lies. Be aware of and manipulate your behavior.

June 12th

All we have is here and now.

We live in the infinite present, however, our brain creates shortcuts and puts us on autopilot, both of which takes us out of the present. Think about it, do you pay attention when you lock your door or when you drive? It's not a bad thing as it frees up resources to engage in more complex things. There are no problems with these shortcuts as long as they are done in the right doses.

How do we know when we are not mentally here? We start worrying about "Did I lock the door?" "Where did I park?" "Did I take my credit card back from the cashier?" These questions remind us that we need to pay more attention to the here and now and that we must slow down.

Be in the present moment, it's the only place we live.

June 13th

Western culture tends to look at things in a binary way. There is either good or bad, you're with me or against me. There are good people and there are bad people. It's a superficial paradigm that creates unnecessary hostility and tension. Is there really just good and bad? And if there was, why would you be the one to judge? Is good and bad just a point of view? Is a lion who eats a goat bad? Would it be better for the lion to pity their prey and starve to death instead? This black and white paradigm creates tension between partners since one is always right and the other wrong. But, no one has monopoly over the good, over being right, or logical. It's all just perspective and how we see the world.

Instead of being judgmental, learn to enjoy what's there and take responsibility for your responses to things. This way, we're open to the differences between us and learn more about the world and ourselves. Try it, it's worth it.

June 14th

Spiritual growth is something that everyone should strive for. I can defend this statement since it comes from personal experience.

Caution! Before beginning spiritual growth and its happy side effects consult yourself. Side effects include compassion, living in the present moment, happiness, peace, calmness, empowerment, love, responsibility, and gratitude. If you start to feel some of these side effects we recommend continuing with personal and spiritual growth.

Unlike regular medication, the goal is to have as many side effects as possible.

June 15th

How many times have we denied our desires?

Sometimes we give up and prevent ourselves from fulfilling our deepest desires. We allow ourselves to believe that we are doomed to fail because others who are greater than ourselves have failed.

The decision to take action is a significant and formative moment in your life. It's the decision to act for yourself, to listen to your inner voice, to finally believe in yourself, to fulfill yourself and to realize that you are God's greatest creation. You will no longer feel alone, there is a power that's been whispering to you, but you've been too distracted to hear it. It was always there, patient and caring, whispering even when you didn't listen.

It's time to fulfill the desires of your heart. Listen to the whispers with your whole self. It's the truest voice and it wants only the best for you and from you.

June 16th

In George Orwell's novel *Animal Farm* he writes, "Animals are equal, but some animals are more equal than others." The same could be said of humans.

It was certainly true when socio-economic classes were perpetuated. Your destiny was determined at birth when you were either born as a son of nobility or as a sharecropper's daughter who was doomed to work the lands of the rich.

This situation no longer holds. The digital revolution has created an infinite amount of opportunities. For the first time in history everyone finally gets a chance at a piece of the pie. The number of millionaires and billionaires making their fortunes online or through social media is astounding. Nowadays, if you're talented enough you can beat the big ones at their own games. There's no shortage of examples. Today, more than ever, you can fulfill your dreams in ways others have only imagined. The number of tools at your disposal weren't even available to kings less than a hundred years ago. The realization of your potential is almost effortless!

June 17th

Courage is the most effective remedy for fear.

Fear accompanies us throughout our lives, right from the moment of birth. The fear of failing is ingrained in us and over the years other types of fears join in. The first fears we experience are justified, as their purpose is to alert us to situations of danger and prevent us from taking unwise risks. Over the years, however, we carry around unnecessary fear that burdens us. It's incredible how many things we refrain from doing because fear has taken our strength. Most people don't regret the things they did, but the things they don't do. Whether it's the partner who got away, not asking for a pay raise, or some other missed opportunity due to fear and feeling inferior, you have denied yourself greatness.

If we let fear run us then we have achieved fear's goal. We need to shine the spotlight on courage, the emotion that will bring us to the next level. Courage doesn't give up easily. It's your job to let courage bravely ward off fear and so you can run the show the way you want. Be courageous right now and let it lead you. Fear won't give up easily so be sure to leave it far behind.

Be brave!

June 18th

The universe isn't against us. It simply isn't interested in us. Our existence is random. We are one person out of billions. This isn't to say that we shouldn't have rules. There are universal laws like gravity, centrifugal force, the law of attraction, etc.

We have the power to create. Billionaires have realized this and used their power of thought and creativity to build these mega companies that affect all of our lives. This was also done in a relatively short time. Facebook has only been around since 2004. Before Facebook became a social media sensation it was just a thought in some student's mind.

We all have the forces of creation and thought within us, not just the rich and famous. Send the universe your vision and believe in it. Believe that it's possible and think positively, the universe will listen. Practice creating positive thoughts to become a more positive person.

June 19th

Sometimes we plan to do something later on, but when the long-awaited moment arrives we give up.

It's fine if it happens from time to time because in the end we are only human and need to find balance in our lives, but once it becomes a habit it hinders our growth. Our comfort zone is addicting, and a waste of time. Ask yourself, "What do I need to do now?" Not, "What do I want now?" because what we'll want to do is relax and stay in our comfort zone. By answering "What do I need to do?" it will answer the question of what you truly want. For example, suppose you were planning to change into gym clothes and for a run when you returned home from work. What you want to do is run. However, when you get home you'll just feel like laying on the couch. So, what do you need to do? Exactly what you wanted a few hours ago! Get up and go for a run!

Make doing what you need to do a habit and you'll grow into someone who doesn't give up on themselves. The bonus is developing strength.

June 20th

When planning for a long term goal you must ask yourself, "What do I want?"

As children we wanted lots of things, but as we got older and discovered that life wasn't black and white but a variety of colors. Sometimes we abandon what we want because it isn't possible or it isn't the right time, etc. The way to persevere and bring back passion is by asking the strategic question, "What do I want?" For example, I want to be a writer. From there I move on to planning the steps required to move forward with this goal. We need to constantly ask ourselves what we need.

As I mentioned before there's a joke about a man who desperately wanted to win the lottery. Every day before going to bed he prayed to God. The angels saw that this man was always praying so they approached God and asked why his prayer wasn't answered. God said that he terribly wanted to give this man the winning lottery ticket, but the problem was that man never bought one!

Do you understand? This man very much wanted to win the lottery, but he never actually took the steps to help make it happen. You too can want a lot of things, but first ask yourself what you need. If you want to run a marathon but come home after work and decide to lay on the couch that's because you're fulfilling your momentary wants. Ask yourself, "What do I need to do now to fulfill my dream?" The answer would be to go for a run.

Persevere to ensure that you get what you truly want.

June 21ᵗʰ

What's special about this day? For me it's the day my father would drive to the beach and watch the sunset. This day is a turning point. It's the day with the most light and it's also the shortest day of the year in the southern hemisphere. My dad soaked up this day as much as he could.

This is the day you invite the light in, letting it penetrate you and fill you with energy and love. It is also the first day of summer. And no, I didn't forget Australia and their neighbors in the southern hemisphere. For you it's the 21st... of December.

This day is an opportunity to open your heart and absorb the energy of life from the sun. Let's take advantage of this day. Be grateful for all the good there is.

Take a deep breath and be in the present moment!

June 22ᵗʰ

Let's learn to trust ourselves.

It's easy to lean on others and let them choose for us to get rid of our distress. However, this comes at a high price. We are leaving our destiny in the hands of others where their choices will serve themselves first, even if they have a pure heart.

The answers to our questions are inside us. We just have to learn to look inside and listen to the answer. They stem from us, are authentic and independent from anything external.

June 23th

Don't look at the packaging, but at what's inside.

Today packaging has become so pretty and visually pleasing that we forget about its contents. Stunning packaging often hides shallow or damaged products. The biggest example can be found in grocery stores. Cheap imported candy and average chocolate is packaged in luxurious velvet boxes. Unremarkable alcohol is put in spectacular bottles. This extravagance hides a bitter truth, no matter how good it looks. Carcinogenic food coloring and unnecessary preservatives are used to make the candy look better than it is even though it wreaks havoc on children's bodies. Alcohol is disguised in luxury bottles and is nothing but poison that destroys the liver, families and lives. This is all served to us gift wrapped.

Don't be tempted to look at the exterior, look inside. The way products are presented is not an accident. Companies meticulously plan how to advertise their products, whatever the cost to humanity.

June 24ᵗʰ

The food we eat determines our quality of life.
Western food is mostly industrialized and contains ingredients that preserve the contents of a can for as long as possible. The industry produces beautiful, brightly colored food. For this to occur, artificial additives are needed to give these natural foods unnatural properties. Flawless conformed beauty and infinite preservation have a price that most of us pay through diabetes, obesity, heart attacks, strokes, cancer or a thousand other undiscovered illnesses. As with everything, we must seek balance. Someone living in a western country will have a hard time adopting a healthy lifestyle since a bulk of the food that they purchase is from their nearest supermarket, which probably has low quality processed food. So, what can be done?

Besides increasing water intake, the next step would be to incorporate more raw foods such as fruits and vegetables (organic if possible), nuts, legumes, and whole grains into our diets. Begin by looking at food labels and considering the rule of Twelve. While reading the food label count the number of ingredients. If the number exceeds 12 put the product back on the shelf and choose another. If the nutritional label lists sugar or high fructose corn syrup as the first or second ingredient (ingredients are displayed in descending order) then that product goes back on the shelf. Spend less time looking at the box design and more time exploring what's inside.

Give it a try! These are small changes that over the years will contribute to your overall well-being! Pennies in your pocket become dollars in the bank, just as a few healthy ingredients over time becomes a healthy lifestyle.

June 25th

You can distill the essence of any subject material into one sentence.

For example, science of economics was created to combat problems of scarcity, lack of money, raw materials, manpower, etc. If I was asked to encapsulate the study of finance into two words I would say, compound interest.

The power behind compound interest is that it creates a lot of value over time. Saving money every month is possible if you limit unnecessary spending. These savings will grow into a significant amount of money over time with compound interest. These savings will save you since there will always be financial uncertainty and job security is an illusion. You must always save money for yourself, your children and your family. It will pay off and become a necessary safety net. I have experienced how saving has saved me. I have also seen how bad finances can lead to depression, anxiety and familial damage.

Save and start immediately, your future self will thank you.

June 26th

For two decades I've managed investments for clients. I've worked for a number of different companies during my career. It took me a few years to understand something I'd been told all my life, and that was to learn how to trust myself no matter what. I remember sitting in meetings where analysts would come with all their knowledge about other companies and tell us whether we should purchase their securities or sell what we had instead. These analysts came with a target price that they wanted us to pay. Not only did the analysts know everything there was to know about a company, they also knew what the company was worth. The analysts were so smart and yet, so often wrong.

Numerous times I have anticipated that a stock price would go in a completely different direction than the analyst said. So I started referring to these analysts as consultants which allowed me to put less meaning on their calculated numbers. I made the hard decisions based on my own analysis and it didn't work too bad. I'd learned to trust myself and made investment decisions regardless of what the "analysts" said. I remind myself often that "no one has a monopoly on knowledge." It's no different with governments or great leaders when it comes to making mistakes; and sometimes their mistakes seem so stupid... you know why? Because they're only human, even if we expect them to be much more. I remember an interview with Steve Ballmer, CEO of Microsoft, who was laughing about the iPhone craze in 2007. "Who'd pay $700 for something like that?" The rest is history.

We have the ability to achieve what we want. The information we need is easy to get so there's nothing else to do except trust our abilities and make the right decisions.

June 27th

Do you ever wonder why fear and doubt pops up at the very worst times, like when you finally are presented with an opportunity? Why is it that, when you are ready to step up to the next level, your frailest emotions swoop in and make you retreat?

When it happens the next time, ask yourself why. Why are fear and doubt interfering right now? Are they there to protect you? To prevent self-actualization that will elevate you and weaken them? Do these frail emotions serve you or themselves?

Fearlessness and bravery are required to ask and answer these questions. Deal with fear and doubt, they have no place in your growth. They will come, it's in their nature. Contain and embrace them. Tell them that their services are no longer needed.

June 28th

Sometimes we find ourselves stuck on an unresolved matter that becomes an obsession. As we delve deeper into the problem the solution becomes farther away. We feel exhausted, drained of energy and our thoughts are empty.

The solution will come! Wait patiently. Let the magic happen. It will take time, but thankfully doesn't depend on active thought. We can do it in our sleep. The way to help is to stop helping. One day, out of nowhere, the solution you've so longed for will be there.

Be patient and remember that it isn't always possible to make things become what they're not ready to be.

June 29th

"All the world's a stage" said Shakespeare in one of his most famous plays, and we are the actors. Most of us fail to realize that we've taken on a certain role. We often live life as if we have no control.

At the end we'll laugh at the fact that we took life so seriously and fell apart over nonsense. Everything seems personal to the ego that fights so hard to win, even at the cost of its own destruction. Life has many theatrical stages and we play a role on certain stages. If we want to change then we need to move to another stage. We'd done it many times before in a light-hearted unconscious way, before we even realized it was even in our power; when we were kids full of curiosity and life. Waking up was magical and full of wonder. We moved from game to game eager to explore with enthusiasm.

The enthusiasm didn't die, it was buried. Our role is to let that enthusiasm rise back up. Reconnect with your erupting joy and experience life as children again. Life should always be fun :-)

June 30th

In an interview with an international Israeli singer, Dana International, she was asked how she managed to cope with her success, publicity and the accompanying pressures. She replied that she reinvents herself every morning.

Are we defined by our past? Is that what we want? Is it possible to break free from the shackles of the past? Why should we bring suffering into our lives today because of what happened years ago? Do we have to bear the baggage of trauma? Why not take the same constructive approach Dana International does and reinvent ourselves every day? The past does not determine who we can be in the future. The past shaped us, but right now we need to look at the present and ask ourselves who we want to be today. There are two emotions that feed on the past: resentment and remorse. Their presence makes it impossible to live in the moment, away from the past. The result is a waste of our inherent potential. We need a full dose of awareness in order to break free.

Awareness makes it possible to break free from the past, let go, forgive and fill the space with new joy that already exists in us.

July

July 1st

Ultimately, the responsibility is all ours.
We will always find ourselves in tough situations, but the choices that we consciously or unconsciously make are the ones that determine our path. We will face many crossroads and we must ask ourselves whether the choices we make will help us grow. If you've chosen the direction of growth, is it accompanied by fear, worry, helplessness or lack of faith?

We must also remember that life's opportunities expand or shrink according to our degree of courageousness, so be brave. Sometimes we'll be lost and won't be able to see very far ahead, but if we've chosen well we can trust the path we've taken.

It's easy to compromise and accept less than what we deserve. We take solace in our comfort zone, especially when our self-belief and self-confidence has abandoned us. So be brave and only choose what helps you grow. How do we know what the right path is? Search for the one that has you feeling enthusiastic and scared!

Today, consciously choose things that challenge and excite you. Practice choosing the scary choice and see how your path changes and leads you to better places.

July 2nd

What are you thinking about?

Our thoughts ultimately determine who we are. Most thoughts are hidden, but that doesn't mean they don't exist. Thoughts are born in us. They exist from the moment we come into the world. Most of the time we don't notice them because they're habitual like breathing. They don't stop for even a moment. So shouldn't we devote some time to our thoughts? We can listen to them, rework them and learn about ourselves.

There is no doubt that our thoughts turn into emotions and then actions. Our hidden and silent thoughts have created the past, present and future for us! They've created who we are. If we want to become something else (healthy, slimmer, richer), then we must change our thoughts. We need to inspire ourselves into action, which will then allow the future that we want to take shape. As long as we let the constant stream of thoughts flow without conscious involvement, we will most likely end up somewhere other than our intended destination.

From now on the responsibility is ours. I invite you to dedicate a few minutes of daily solitude to listen to your thoughts and make conscious decisions about what you want and how to get there.

July 3rd

We have a lot of reasons to be frustrated.

When we wake up we're already a little frustrated from the lack of sleep. On the road there could be a torrential downpour or an accident that's holding up traffic. The road is just one big annoying traffic jam and there are lines everywhere with nowhere to pull off. And what about our partner? They never do what we ask just to frustrate us on purpose. In general, it's frustrating when people don't do what we ask of them or act like we expect them to. This list is long and it gets longer minute by minute while the frustration keeps growing.

The whole "when life piles up" situation is nothing new. Control is an illusion and the only thing we can control is our attitude. We are given an opportunity to choose between being an eternal victim who passively watches external forces hurt us, or taking responsibility and learning to connect and dance with reality. It's a surrender to the good and bad of life. We can choose to accept it and be satisfied or go against it and be frustrated.

Today, practice cultivating patience and peace. You'll have many opportunities to do so. Humbly accept any situation and choose to take responsibility for your actions and reactions.

July 4ᵗʰ

Let it go.

Sometimes it's necessary, especially when we're in a "crisis" and it seems like there's no solution that isn't frustrating. Who isn't familiar with these situations, where we feel like we've fallen down a slippery slope and we've lost our breath and all we see is a wall? It could be an argument with a partner that slowly gains momentum and escalates quickly, something that we don't purposefully aim for. It could also be an argument from road rage, or with a close friend or family member which ended in destruction.

A cosmic rule is that as easy as it is to build things, it's always easier to destroy them. An analogy could be building a house of cards. It takes a lot of time and accuracy to build it, but once the first card comes out of place, the others fall at a dizzying speed. This rule also applies to life.

So, what can be done? First, we must understand that our Ego runs the show, it plays a great part in our lives and allows us to express ourselves clearly and feel powerful. However, if we don't learn to restrain it, it can also create destruction around us. So pay attention to your Ego, especially when you're in an argument, and observe how quickly you are filled with anger and rage. That's the Ego talking and your job is to stop it. It's driven by the saying, "The end justifies the means" and it only sees the victory in front of it without considering the cost. The best way is to simply let go. It's hard sometimes, excruciating even, but the reward is definitely worth it.

Letting go is basically deciding that you will take responsibility for the situation and stop the deterioration of it. You must step away from the fighting arena and promise to solve it another time in a better environment.

July 5ᵗʰ

Sleep is more important than you think.

Over the last century the number of hours spent sleeping has shortened significantly. Today the modern man is content with less than seven hours of sleep. Compare that to the nine hours we required in the early 20th century. Some people even believe that sleep is a waste of time.

Modern life, with the need to perform endless tasks, has made sleep a redundant task. But this couldn't be further from the truth. The sensory overload that comes with living in society and all the chores and exhaustion makes it necessary to take a break. Sleep helps us process information, rest and gain strength. Beyond the biological need to sleep, it is a time for your subconscious to process the information you've learned from the day, organize it, and prepare you for the next coming day.

July 6th

Often the results are different from what we want.
That's all right, and though it's not perfect it is natural. Every result begins with the seeds of a thought. What were those thoughts? What thoughts were transformed into final decisions, choices, behaviors and actions? Were you aware of them? Are they your responsibility or others?

As we've already discussed, the mind constantly creates thoughts. Large parts of them are hidden like an iceberg with only the tip accessible for us to see. Therefore, if we want to improve our situations and bring more miracles into our lives we must be responsible for our thoughts. We must cultivate them like a garden encouraging all the positive thoughts to bloom and weeding out the negative ones. If we do that it's guaranteed that our efforts will show through results. Be sure to make small and slow changes so that you don't give yourself mental paralysis.

Start now. Listen to your thoughts and gently replace the negative with positive ones. Good results will come shortly, be confident!

July 7th

We get up in the morning, hurry with our business and repeat.
Some of us aren't happy with our lives. We ask ourselves how
we got to this point. A collection of the decisions we've made
in our lives brought us here. Most likely a large percentage of
the choices we've made didn't have a deliberate path toward
a better future. This is how we find ourselves in an endless rat
race. Weeks pass by. Our dreams are formed by the passing of
time. We live in a movie. Life is a movie. William Shakespeare
described it in the play *As You Like It*, "All the world's a stage,
and all the men and women merely players: they have their ex-
its and entrances; and one man in his time plays many parts."
Who is the writer of our life? If not us, then who? Why don't
we become the writers of our life? Why don't we write our movie? We're the main actors at the forefront of the stage. It's up
to us to pick our supporting cast and which script we want to
perform. Every day we move forward scene by scene. It's time
we became the director *and* the writer. At first it will be difficult
since we're used to leaving everything up to coincidence or a
higher power, but we've seen the results when our leadership
lacks... quite disappointing.
Starting today take the reins and be the writer of your own life.

July 8th

If you have nothing good to say about yourself don't say anything at all.

Not always being at our best is part of being human. We don't always have the desire to communicate and our mood isn't always good. It just happens and everything is still okay. But we find ourselves slipping into negative thought patterns about ourselves and we forget the one basic truth; that everything is fine.

This is life: a roller coaster ride with twists, butterflies in your stomach, nausea, yelling, laughter, joy and happiness. Although the route taken is unique for each person the rules for everyone are the same. Sooner or later we'll go downward and our stomachs will flip, but after a while we'll climb back up. That's life's pattern. We must understand and internalize that this is the way things are. Sometimes when we're down negative thoughts will creep in and lead us into the abyss. The easiest and simplest way to stop these thoughts is to believe that there is room for only one thought at a time, and it better be positive! All we need to do is take responsibility, grab the reins during the steep descent and replace our negative thoughts with one simple mantra, a true and genuine mantra. Say it until it becomes part of you and say it out loud: I love myself!

July 9th

If you never ask... the answer will always be no!

Too often we want to ask a question or a favor but for different reasons we swallow our tongue and avoid asking. Often these questions require a hint of courage. We prefer to avoid asking our boss for a raise. We avoid asking our relatives for favors so that we don't seem weak or rude. The ego has too much pride and it doesn't want any help.

Each question or request ultimately has only two answers: yes or no. Let go of the assumption that if you don't ask the question the answer is already no. Asking a question or for a favor will ultimately improve our situation. Simply be brave and ask the question, the worst thing that can happen is that the answer will be no. So, what are you waiting for?! Ask your questions today and see what happens. The worst-case scenario is that you'll get a no!

Be aware of this! Ask questions or ask for favors when it's difficult. This is where the growth happens. The more you practice the easier it gets.

July 10th

Every day is a new opportunity. History has been written and our memories remain, but that is past. The advantage of a new day is that we can reinvent ourselves. It's not coincidental that we sleep each night, it's an opportunity for us to pause, leave yesterday behind and start again when we wake. A well-known saying discusses remembering the past, dreaming of the future, but living only in the present. The present is this moment – now. Each day is open to a world of opportunities. Every morning we're reborn and we should create the day in the best possible way. Even if there are some loose ends or unfinished business from yesterday, we still have time to choose another approach or a different attitude and find compassion for ourselves in stressful situations. It's a new morning, so make it a *good* morning!

Consciously decide to have a good day. Remember that your attitude is what counts.

July 11th

It is often better to jump off the cliff and into the water than standing by and watching others go.
We'll never be completely ready. We'll lack knowledge about one thing or another and feel unprepared to make moves. We will wish that we had more time and knowledge, meanwhile others, perhaps less talented people, will move forward while we stay stuck struggling with self-doubt. If we keep waiting for the perfect moment to make a move we'll find that we've missed the train.

We'll only ever be 80% ready and that's fine. We will never have enough time to be 100% ready. It's action that shapes our path, not the time we take getting ready to do it. Preparation can become an addiction that keeps us trapped and tells us that we're not ready. We must break this vicious cycle by understanding its role in our lives and by breaking our limitations even if we aren't perfectly ready. Action defines us and offers us growth. If it's not perfect it's okay. Perfection is not available to humans.

So, get going!

July 12th

It struck me one day while I was riding the bus...

I was leaning against the window looking out. The view was stunning and meditative in the busy city. I thanked the driver for driving smoothly while I was staring out the window mesmerized by the road. There was something soothing about it. When the bus had reached the station people hurried to their destinations. Opposite me, I saw a young girl leaning against and looking out her window, the same as I. Mirror images of meandering minds we spotted each other. It struck me like lightning that we looked at our world through glass, seeing but never reaching out to touch. This, of course, is a metaphor but so much do we stare at reality without seeing it. Other times we keep ourselves at a safe distance protected by glass, never really participating as more than a spectator in the game of life.

The bus drives on and life passes by. Our choices are to either let it pass by untouched or fully participate in it. I don't mean to sound cliche, I am hoping to bring awareness. You deserve to experience the whole range of emotions; surrender to pain, love, be happy, face fears, live each moment and wrap yourself in its warmth. Understand yourself that everything is fine and it's supposed to be that way. You deserve it.

July 13th

Baz Luhrmann the Australian film director, screenwriter and producer of hits like *Moulin Rouge*, wrote a song based on his personal life about his struggle with depression. The song, "Everybody's Free (To Wear Sunscreen)" was released in 1998 and hit the charts with-a-bullet. Baz's song opens with golden advice:

"If I could offer you only one tip for the future,
sunscreen would be it
A long-term benefits of sunscreen have been proved by scientists
Whereas the rest of my advice has no basis more reliable
Than my own meandering experience,
I will dispense this advice now."

There is no doubt that this song influenced many to wear sunscreen, but that was never the point of the song. It's that there's not much we can do to change our lives except for the simple little things, like sunscreen.

If I had to distill all that I know about finance, which is my career, I would say that the eighth wonder of the world is compound interest! Albert Einstein said, "Compound interest is the eighth wonder of the world. He who understands it, earns it; he who doesn't, pays it."

The secret is its simplicity. So my advice is to save. Save your pennies and your bank will take care of itself, with the help of compound interest of course. Save a fixed amount every month, no matter what. Forget about that money and act as if it isn't yours.

Do it for your future self and then save the same way for your children. Compound interest will stand by you.

July 14th

Mahatma Gandhi's famous words were, "Be the change that you wish to see in the world." This used to be so unimaginable to me, it clashed with my human nature. The ego within me demanded that the things around me needed to change. Super Ego didn't accept my wife's behavior and demanded that she change. It whispered in my ear, "you think she's changed, but she hasn't at all." Super Ego judges and criticizes. What do we get out of that other than lots of frustration because the world refuses to change?

Before I understood what Gandhi meant, circumstances seemed unfair, uncomfortable and not the way I wanted. The universe didn't influence how I felt. The only one responsible for my feelings was me, so I changed them. I began to work on myself and watched how the world reacted to me. Over time, with the changes in consciousness and attitude, external change began to happen. Pressure, judgment and criticism were replaced with compassion, acceptance, inclusion and love. With this skill set, values and perceptions, who could tell you no? I highly recommend that you adopt this approach as well to life because there's not much you can change outside of you. Everything will work out.

July 15th

I recently went to a funeral.

It was a sad celebration of a life I wasn't expecting to end so soon. My beloved aunt passed away. She had just celebrated the Bat Mitzvah of my oldest daughter two weeks before. Her death caught us all by surprise. Although my aunt wasn't young, she seemed to have a lot of life left in her.

My aunt was admitted to the hospital a few days before her passing. She had difficulty breathing. The doctors read the results of several tests and then informed her sons that she was in the final stages of muscular dystrophy and her entire respiratory system was shutting down. Her lungs were so weak that she could no longer breathe on her own. My aunt made the brave decision to not fight against it. Her three sons and relatives were given a few days to organize themselves and say goodbye. We were all faced with both her courage, grace and greatness and the loss of her- the woman we all loved.

Today I saw her buried. Her body was just a shell that was lowered into the ground at a graveyard where other family members rest. In the distance I heard the roar of traffic, trucks rushing down the highway and cars honking to pass. The metallic hum was contrasted by the silence of the cemetery. In that moment of holiness, a thought echoed in my soul that everything is possible, in the fullest sense of the word. Eventually, all of our journeys will end and we'll be forgotten because the world won't stop for us. All the good deeds, the less than good, the fears, and doubts will disappear forever. Why does what we do or think matter? Why not use our time to live our lives in the way they were meant to be lived: fully? One day this struggle will end and when it does, we'll be judged by one thing only: whether or not we've lived the lives that our Creator gifted us with!

July 16th

Everyone admires musicians.

Who doesn't have a favorite singer and song? Tickets for concerts sell out fast around the world. Music has a magical unifying power. Many songs are about love, hope, and fulfillment. In fact, singing can be seen as a kind of a prayer. When we sing we feel united. Our moods improve and sometimes our emotions get the better of us and our eyes fill with tears that express our inner soul.

Why not use the power of music and poetry to feed ourselves positive messages? The power of prayer is much like the power of poetry. Try humming powerful lyrics in your head, like a prayer, and let your inner chant take you away. Let your musical prayer produce gratitude, love and hope.

Life can be much more beautiful if we sing it. So sing inside your heart, be grateful and feel love.

July 17th

It's amazing how things work out.
I'd like to share what happened to me two hours ago. A good friend of mine wanted me to join him while he purchased his first apartment and secured his ideal mortgage plan. I willingly agreed to go and I offered to help him with his financial endeavors, free of charge. My gift was considerable. My friend insisted on paying but I refused. His wife, who was also there, offered her services as a web designer and talented graphic artist to rework my website since I'd mentioned earlier that it was something that I needed to do. While my website wasn't a top priority it was comforting to know that the improvements would be made out of kindness and not for profit. Somehow, I felt my friend's desire to give back would make this a work of love and not business, thereby producing a better product.

Generosity is a gift that everyone deserves, when it is given it is also gained. I helped my friend with housing and in return my website's viewing rates were higher after his wife's redesign. Trading skills to achieve success is a win-win situation for all.

July 18th

What are your goals?

A common example of this, and I suppose many will relate, was when I wanted to lose weight. I set weight goals for myself and sometimes I achieved them and sometimes I didn't. After a while I realized that wanting to lose weight must be a symptom of a bigger goal, so I sat and thought about why I actually wanted to lost weight. I realized that it was because I wanted a healthier lifestyle so that I could live longer. Since that day I've focused on sports, proper nutrition, meditation and stress-free living. I've added muscle and lost fat all without weighing myself or counting calories. Another example is when I wanted to be a better dad. At first, I sat and thought about smaller goals I could do to achieve this big goal like taking my girls for bike rides on the weekend or doing other small outings or activities that we could enjoy together. But when I thought about why I wanted to do all of those things I realized that what I really wanted was for us all to be happier. I wanted peace, calmness, self-respect, self-love and gratitude towards my children. Without noticing, while working towards those smaller goals, my daughters' lives changed for the better. Amazing, isn't it?

So, what are your big goals and which of your values do you want to portray?

July 19th

Trust yourself.

You're much smarter than you think. It took me a while to figure this one out. I'm with myself day and night and I know myself as best I can. It's true that it's easy to trust others, but their concern is with themselves. Trust yourself because it's the right thing to do, because you know yourself truly and sincerely. It may be difficult at first. Accept that everyone is unique and special. You're fine as you are and there is nothing to fix. You're smart and you know what's best for you.

So be brave and dive in. You won't regret it.

July 20th

"Scientia Potentia Est" or "Knowledge is Power".

Sir Francis Bacon, a philosopher, is commonly attributed to this famous saying, even though there's no clear evidence that he ever said it. However, the sentiment is correct, knowledge *is* power. This belief causes students to thirst after knowledge. Knowledge allows humanity to continue growing and break through its own boundaries to reinvent itself.

However, knowledge alone isn't enough. We occasionally come across really S*mart* (with a capital S) people. They are the people that are walking encyclopedias, but when it comes to their personal lives, they don't have a single clue on how to be satisfied. We'd expect someone so Smart to be able to figure things out, but oftentimes the knowledge that they have is stored away in their minds somewhere, never to be acted upon. Knowledge is power only if it's translated into action. The application of knowledge is the real power!

Remember to always strive for knowledge and always apply that knowledge to your life. Incorporate what you learn into how you live. Give your knowledge value.

July 21th

Know your weaknesses.

Remember that we're human and as such we have been blessed with strengths and also (for the sake of balance) weaknesses. Society does everything it can to appear perfect. Weaknesses are not highlighted; they are presented as something negative and as something to be fixed (with a lot of money) or hidden. We become frustrated when tremendous efforts are made to hide our weaknesses whether it's through physical, mental or behavioral changes.

Hold your fork like this. Lose weight and tuck your tummy in. Smile, be confident, show interest, shake your depression off, etc. The energy needed to hide these things is so immense that we feel exhausted and dissatisfied at the end of the day. But why fix what isn't broken? We're human and our weaknesses aren't bad or negative. We need to accept them and not try to hide or fix them. Freedom and freshness come into our lives when we embrace our weaknesses. Accept them as something human and natural.

What are your weaknesses that you hide and what would you gain if you choose to accept them?

July 22th

Be whole with your actions.

Align your actions with your values.

It's meaningful because it connects to your values and the core of your soul. Choose to live with responsibility for your actions and without feeling the need to owe others explanations. This will allow yourself true expression of freedom and will let you clearly see your goals and work towards achieving them.

Choose wisely, choose from wholeness and recognize your value. It stems from knowing yourself. Always strive for it.

July 23th

Think about how fun it would be to give up control and fear and just surrender.

In devotion there's quiet acceptance of reality. There's nothing to fix, everything is fine. Practice devotion to love. Love someone without expecting anything in return, just give of yourself.

Pain is part of the deal. There is no distancing yourself from or avoiding pain out of fear; this is the essence of devotion, to accept and embrace the unknown with peace. Dedicate yourself to life and what it has to offer. Everything is fine and nothing is personal or against us. Dedicate yourself and powerfully experience pain, love and life. Surrender to this moment. And this moment and this one. This is life with happiness and humility. It's so much fun. Practice it every moment, it's worth it. Don't seek reward, don't seek justice or "what I deserve".

Dedicate yourself without reward and feel life flowing through you. Live in the present moment and surrender all of yourself. Everything is fine.

July 24th

When was the last time you said thank you?

I mean truly not automatically? I hope you've incorporated this into your daily life. Studies about happiness have concluded that saying thank you, appreciation and gratitude makes us happier. But we already know this from books, articles and videos. I invite you to practice saying thank you and smile a smile of gratitude.

It's easy to complain about our boss, the one who doesn't understand, who is cold and unsympathetic, but no matter how you look at it, the boss is the one providing you with your livelihood. Maybe it's an imperfect spouse. Even if you think they don't deserve to be told thank you, tell them anyway. It doesn't have to be to their face, you can say it internally. Be grateful and say thank you. You'll slowly notice change, something new is happening. I do this for my business and I notice that this practice is much stronger than any marketing or advertising. I don't do this out of greed for money but out of gratitude as my business provides me and my family with respect and therefore I'm incredibly thankful.

Every day give it a little thought. Stop for a moment, close your eyes and say thank you.

July 25th

So many distractions.
Whether it's when we're driving, listening to the news or on public transportation the advertisements never stop. No wonder so many people arrive at work already exhausted. We're unknowingly exposed to about a million commercials a year. That means we're intaking about 3,000 advertisements a day. Is it any wonder that there's unease and addiction to consumption? We've become addicted to background noises and noise pollution. It's so easy to lose concentration today.

Find a few minutes of quiet time for yourself every day. It's not a waste of time, it's taking advantage of time. It will only do you good.

July 26th

I want to share something that just happened to me.

I was talking to a company owner whom I provided training services for. Due to an opportunity, I had announced the termination of our contract. Contractually, this isn't a breach as I informed him with enough notice. He was uneasy and tried to stay matter-of-fact. I contained his anger and didn't waiver in my goal of improving my life and doing what is best for me without hurting others. We're surrounded by a sea of interests and desires. Wherever you go, you're probably stepping on someone's toes. Through all of this you need to stay true to yourself because ultimately the path is yours. People will come and go.

Remember, this is your life. Live it as you wish. There will be enough people who will try to dissuade you, but you must stand up for your right to choose, and for your destiny and future. There will always be people who will try to prevent you from doing things that will help you reach your goal. It's not personal, that's just their job. Your job is to overcome these people and be true to yourself.

July 27ᵗʰ

Today, we will address the power of repetition.

This book tries to address a new insight every day, and it's impossible to do this without overlapping other insights. I'm reminded of a workshop I once attended on "The Power of Positive Thinking" where one student told the instructor that the subject material was similar to that of the "Relationships" lecture. The instructor replied that ultimately, he didn't have anything new to say, we already knew everything we needed to know about life. The instructor stated that his job was to help us apply what we already knew to our lives, and one way to do that was to repeat the same message over and over again. Repetition plays a crucial role in shaping new patterns of behavior and spiritual growth. You've probably heard of the saying, "Practice makes perfect."

So today, use the law of repetition and tell yourself, "I love myself" over and over until it sticks, and then have a lovely day!

July 28th

In truth, we all have the potential for spiritual greatness.
Sometimes there is darkness that separates us from our potential, shielding our greatness for a "better" time to be revealed. The dark abyss floods us with fears, doubts, and worries, leaving no room for goodness. John Wooden said, "Don't let what you cannot do interfere with what you can do."

We place most of the obstacles on our path to success, but we must not allow ourselves to interfere with the person that we can become. There are no limits other than those that we have set for ourselves.

July 29th

I wrote this while hiking.

Today is Saturday, the winter sun is warming me up as I hike. I feel its pleasant rays across my face as I inhale the greenery. I reach a small stream of water. I ponder at how the waterfall was created and remember something I once heard that's doubly true at this moment. "Many of us are required to reinvent ourselves." The water droplet doesn't carve the rock by strength but by perseverance! Wow how true that is, perseverance is one of the cornerstones of our growth. It's a common force in nature and we humans sometimes refer to it as a burden.

Remember that as a baby perseverance made you walk. You had fallen and risen countless times before you were able to take your first step. Perseverance is a law of nature. Embrace it!

July 30th

Wherever your attention is, is where you will be.

Our stream of thoughts is constant and are usually recurring thoughts. Do yours focus on past regrets or future anxieties? Are you thinking about the fear of missing out or your doubts about the future? Where do you really want to be? What is your vision? Clearly see it in your mind.

Slowly take control of your stream of thoughts and direct it towards your vision, growth, and a better future. Your thoughts flow even when you don't notice so make it a daily practice. Direct your thoughts towards your desires.

July 31ᵗʰ

The weak avenge, the strong forgive and the wise ignore.
Whichever one you choose can help you measure your position on the spirituality scale. Do you have the desire for revenge? It reminds me of a Seinfeld episode where one of the characters, George, who was neurotic, wanted revenge on someone by having a great comeback. After deciding on and delivering his comeback the same man who insulted him in the first place disappointingly had a better comeback that left George speechless. In the final scene of the episode, on his way to the airport, he came up with another comeback. He turned the vehicle around and went back to get revenge.

Revenge doesn't do anything other than satisfy one's inexhaustible ego. We lust to feel victorious but sometimes victory is accompanied by defeat in the form of anger, insults and the destruction of a relationship. A spiritual person will eventually notice the ego and realize that it's just one layer of their personality. They will realize that they are not their ego. A spiritually strong person can train themselves to forgive and will understand that another's behavior stems from their choice, they know they aren't responsible for it. I once heard "Hurt people hurt people." Peaceful people know that revenge is a waste of time and leads to suffering so they choose to forgive and move on with their lives. We're constantly surrounded by people who are always asking for a part of you. It isn't a bad thing, it is what it is and everything is fine. There are those who'll manipulate you to control you and then there are those who'll threaten you. The way you react is your choice.

August

August 1st

A successful and wise old man was once asked how he had managed to keep the same enthusiasm, faith and willpower throughout his entire life.

He simply answered that he reinvented himself every morning. He said that although it's true that not everyone has an easy life, it doesn't matter when it comes to the laws of growth. The laws of growth are to think positively, trust in yourself, be compassionate and fill yourself and the world with love. Remember that everything begins with a single thought and that thought creates your reality. It's a consistent, ongoing process that requires discipline and awareness, but this is your life we are talking about! The past may have brought us here, but that doesn't mean that that's how the future has to be.

You woke up this morning. It's a new day and a new beginning. I understand there may be difficulties, but the choice to be happy or take charge of your day can offer hope. Reinvent yourself! Your choices today impact who you'll be in the future. Let go of the past and break the boundaries that defy you – it's up to you! Figure out your potential, tap into your creative powers and transform the person you are!

August 2nd

Today we'll talk about death.
Is it a terrible thing? Is it the end of the world? Some believe that death is a direct continuation of life, and as much as we want to believe this no one has yet to come back from the dead to tell us that it's true.

Death accompanies us every day, even every hour and can, in the blink of an eye, take our fragile lives. This is just the way things are and that's okay. We were predestined to die and there is nothing we can do to change that. We must learn to accept that death is inevitable both for us and our loved ones. This is the cycle of life. The pain, suffering and feelings of loss will come and no one is immune to it. We can only surrender. We must understand that we can't be here forever. Therefore, we should focus on living the lives we've been given, instead of trying to pass by death.

This means that we must only do the things we want to. Take risks, be creative and brave, and stop being afraid of what might happen because we're going to die anyway. Why not allow ourselves to live a little before we go!

August 3rd

What do we need?

One of the best skills we can have in our consumerist culture is the ability to distinguish between what we require and what we actually need. The advertising machine constantly works and dulls our senses, making us addicted to consumption like a drug. The only way to achieve peace is by consuming more and more. It isn't a bad thing to consume, it's a matter of the degree. We don't need many material goods to feel okay about ourselves. The endless slavery to the new and exciting sentences most of us to a life of misery and poverty. In order to maintain this excessive consumption culture, loans, mortgages, and credit cards have sprung up with promises to fulfill your desires here and now. Are these really desires that are worth enslaving your future for? I ask you to be aware that we're constantly bombarded with advertisements that promise us happiness if we buy this or that. The greatest example of this is when a new phone comes out. The line starts days before the launch. A year later the same phone is as useful as a door stopper. Who would have remembered that only a year ago people slept on the ground outside the store to buy one. We have the responsibility to think about our future and try to create a culture of saving instead of using. There will come a day when we retire and we'll be okay because we've saved and accumulated income over the years. We must always save a part of our income. We may be saving at the cost of buying, but it will ensure a better future!

The best thing you could do for your financial future is to save. If you are not, open a savings account for your retirement. Your future self will thank you.

August 4th

Let your subconscious solve your problems

Sometimes we have certain tasks ahead of us that seem like the more we struggle with it, the further the solution becomes. It can be frustrating, no matter the size of the problem. It could be a small problem we need to solve or a decision we must make with long term consequences (like buying a property, investing in a business etc).

In these situations, it's definitely beneficial to engage with the subconscious, the part working behind the scenes in our minds, comfortably and without distraction. The best way to use this tremendous resource is to think. Focus on the problem and ask the subconscious for help, and then let go. Trust that your subconscious knows how to find its way. The answer will come when it's the right time, sometimes after sleep, exercise or even out of nowhere. Learn how to step away from the problem for a while in order to find the solution.

Practice now. Think of a problem, challenge or obstacle and ask your subconscious for help by gently asking a question internally, and then forget about it. Go on with your business and wait patiently. The answer will ultimately come.

August 5th

Learn to say NO.

The word no can be perceived as something offensive and antisocial. Many avoid saying no and instead use distractions. We were taught that it's impolite to say no. We feel that we should hint at our discontent rather than state it out of respect to the person asking. The culture of political correctness is here so who wants to be seen as rude or impolite? We must be progressive and careful not to over step our boundaries. Telling this white lie is easier than telling the truth.

No is a word that indicates our power and strength. We must rely on ourselves to use this word so that we don't become victims or deceive others. The word no is an assertive statement that clarifies our wants and prevents others from doubting us. There's nothing like saying the simple truth. The word no isn't rejecting the person, but instead rejecting the specific request they are asking!

Don't be afraid to say no if that's your truth. Respect yourself and those around you.

August 6th

Don't forget your constant companion; the angel of death.

Your angel is there to remind you of something important, perhaps something in your daily routine that you often forget.

Problems, worry and exhaustion from the rat race makes us forget a basic but important truth: everything can end at any moment. You've known this your entire life, but have you ever really engaged with that thought? I'm not suggesting that you act without constraint just because the end is near, we were given wisdom to act responsibly.

Part of this wisdom is the knowledge that all living things are here temporarily. We're guests of earth just for a moment and nothing more can be expected. History books are full of leaders and great scientists who changed our world, but aren't alive to enjoy it. Everything is temporary and everything will one day be underground and history.

Life is a miracle, a miracle of creation and we must cherish it every moment of the day. The angel of death accompanies us every step of the way, *they* are our constant companion. There is no place for fear or doubt in the little bit of time that we have, so dare, risk, change and grow! Life can end in a minute so why not try to defeat the fear! What do you have to lose?

Ask yourself *what do I have to lose*? List all possibilities of what could happen if you decided to do something brave today.

August 7th

Love yourself.

We have heard this cliche so many times in our lives. Although it's been over used, the phrase shows the meaning of our purpose. Despite the importance of self-love, it seems that often it's neglected and put in the hands of strangers. We're so thirsty for love from others that we forget we can love ourselves. We've developed so much dependence on external love that we are addicted.

Self-love doesn't depend on anything and we are the only ones truly committed to cherishing and appreciating ourselves. How we look, how much money we have and how successful we are is unimportant and external, these things have nothing to do with our internal self.

Addiction to external love can end in tragedy. I remember a television host in Israel, with whom I grew up with, who was delightful and charismatic. The audience loved him and he became a great success. Over the years the fame began to fade. His ending was bitter; he threatened to kill the producers if they didn't hire him back. He missed the love of his audiences so much that he went too far. The story ended with him committing suicide. Why did he long for this love so deeply? Like with every addiction, the body and soul lose the ability to love themselves and when the "drug" is gone the soul collapses.

Don't walk a path just for love. Learn to accept and love yourself. It's really simple, just be aware of and appreciate your internal life. If you don't learn to love yourself, you'll always depend on the love of others.

While you're walking, sitting or waiting throughout the day, remind yourself that you love yourself. Repeat this sentence until it becomes part of you. Start now!

August 8th

Pretend.

Unpleasant situations which cause defeatist thoughts and lead us to less than perfect outcomes happen to everyone. When it happens, we sometimes discover that we don't have the mental strength to cope. It could be a conversation with our boss, criticism when being evaluated, a conflict with our partner or even a conversation where we weren't able to share our side and left feeling defeated. Sometimes we mean to say one thing but we say something else. If we were the hero we most admire, what would we do? Your hero wouldn't give up. They would stand their ground in an assertive way and take what they deserve.

So pretend!

Practice being your hero. Imagine it, breathe it in slowly and see how the hero becomes you. Become the hero that knows exactly what they want and knows how to get it.

Achieve something small for yourself today, get something you wanted but didn't ask for. Now *you* are the hero and you can have it!

August 9th

Today we'll look at the concept of remorse. My mother-in-law once told me that the main difference between her and I was experience. She'd gained experience by being alive for a few decades longer than me. Experience has a priceless value. The wisdom she'd gained over the years was evident in her eyes. On the other hand, I recall looking at the face of an elderly man and there was a considerable amount of pain in his eyes. Was it the pain of missing out? Maybe it was out of remorse? Or was it just his circumstances or his luck?

The vast majority of people regret the things they didn't do in their lives, not the things they did. It could be missed love, a missed promotion, or a missed opportunity because one wasn't prepared.

In my youth I loved watching *Seinfeld*. One of the characters, George Costanza was a comedic and neurotic character. In one episode he was on his way to the airport pondering what he wanted to say but didn't. George decided to turn the vehicle around so he could go back and say what he should have in the first place. But how many of us would turn the wheel around? How many of us would continue straight on with the feeling of missing out?

The common denominator is fear. Fear creates missed opportunities. However, while fear hurts, it's existence is short and its effects fade. Remorse often accompanies us for decades. A wise saying in the Philippines is, "Fear is temporary, but remorse is permanent." So do yourself a favor and do the right thing, even if it comes wrapped in fear. It could hurt in the short term, but it will pass. Don't let remorse have a permanent place in your soul.

Next time you see an opportunity, accept the fear! It will eventually dissipate.

Strive to be the You that you deserve!

August 10th

"Just yesterday I was a baby" said the elderly father to his son when he was at his deathbed.

Life passes before our eyes because we are in a rat race. The days go by without returning and the tombstone seems closer than ever. It isn't a good thing or bad, it's just a fact. It's our responsibility to interpret this in an empowering way. The constant company of the angel of death by our side can be a wonderful gift, reminding us that life is short and unpredictable. As each day passes and we become older we will understand that nothing happened when we chose a different lane, so why not live life with the understanding that it's only temporary. We alone are responsible for our happiness, and our happiness is reflected in the way we choose to walk every day and hour. It's your responsibility to choose the path of happiness that best suits you. Don't expect someone else to choose for you.

If you understand this you can look at life directly in the eyes and assume that anything is possible if you allow it.

So today, choose to live! Start taking responsibility for your life whether you succeed or fail because in the end we all die, and what's important is that you have lived a meaningful life!

August 11th

Be brave, what do you have to lose?

As far as we know we only live once so why not be brave? Why not dream? Why listen to others? The answers are inside of you. You must be brave and break through your own boundaries, at most you'll succeed.

Do it, you owe it to yourself. Time passes quickly; infancy, childhood, adulthood, seniority and then death. I keep in my heart the title of an article, "Only Yesterday I was a Baby " in which a dying father talks to his son in the hospital and tells him that only yesterday he was a baby and now here he is at the end of his days soon to become stardust.

And you who are reading this now, what are your dreams? Go out and fulfill them. You owe it to yourself. There will be difficulties and objections, but the more you dare to dream the more the environment will create that reality for you.

August 12th

The pursuit of happiness in the Western world is seen as something that requires endless finances.

We are waiting for the next dream vacation, the next new phone, or shopping trips. These are really just small peaks of happiness because the material world doesn't have a lasting effect on happiness. We will be happier for a while and then plummet back down. It's an addiction that forces us to consume more and more. It's not just a symptom, but a cultural marker that has developed into an epidemic. So many find themselves immediately planning their next vacation as soon as the one they are on ends.

Spiritual growth can give us lasting happiness. The work is done behind closed doors, silently and internally. Are poor kids playing football barefoot less happy than their rich friends with shoes? Do they look sad while playing? Absolutely not, sometimes their happiness exceeds those who play on nice grass and branded cleats. Their worries are noticeably small. The simplicity in which they live and the basic needs they are content with allow them to live a carefree life with strong family ties, community and a strong sense of belonging.

Ultimately, we all have the same desire and that is to maximize our happiness. More cars and more toys won't contribute to a rise in happiness. It's changing our thought patterns, transforming our negative thoughts into positive ones and developing our muscle of optimism that will ensure happiness.

There is always internal work to be done. Choose happiness no matter what!

August 13th

Strive to achieve inner peace.

When you achieve it, it will show externally. Sometimes the world seems like a threatening place where our mental or even physical survival is not guaranteed. Some of us feel like we live in war zones. Despite news coverage that highlights the bad and glorifies drama, we are living at a time where personal security is at its peak. A few hundred years ago a village or city could be raided, pillaged and then set on fire with citizens murdered and lives ruined at any moment. Today it's likely that we will pass from old age or illness, not from war. Statistically, longevity is now at its peak, however, it creates the pressing problem of mental survival. Depression today is among the most prevalent illnesses and probably stems from concentrating on the gap between "the desired" and "the existing." This happens until it's unbearable and mental collapse occurs.

The purpose of this book is to focus on our souls where there is light and balance. When we get in touch with our soul, we reflect innocence and truth. Drama is forgotten, dead ends turn into opportunities and life becomes the miracle we believed it was when we were young. Ultimately, peace begins with us. Strive to grow and realize your potential.

Stop caring about what others say. Trust yourself and appreciate yourself. Stand behind the enlightened you.

August 14th

Many of us in the Western world have glasses.

The increase in use of smartphones and TVs disrupt our eyesight. Other than the celebration by optometrists and ophthalmologists who make their hundreds of thousands of dollars off of your myopia, I want to talk to you about your glasses. Not your physical glasses but those through which you see reality. Reality happens through the eyes of the observer. For example, something you may have seen as a disaster could have been a miracle for someone wearing their rose-colored glasses.

I've already shared with you my experience in Crete where I heard one couple complaining about everything from the crowded room, to the weak flow of water, to the cold weather, and the other couple who, when I asked how they were enjoying their holiday, talked about how fantastic it was! It's the same vacation just seen through different pairs of glasses.

Which pair are you going to choose? What do you think about removing your dark glasses in the morning and choosing to wear your other optimistic rose pair instead?

August 15th

French writer Nicolas Champur who lived in the eighteenth century thought of life as a disease and death as a cure.

How shocking. My mother used to say that life is an opportunity. Which do you agree with? Which do you choose? There are those who get up in the morning only because they didn't die during the night. Statistically speaking we aren't supposed to exist at all. Our very existence is a miracle. We had to race against hundreds of millions to the egg and beat them all. What are the chances? Look at life as an opportunity for growth, and empower yourself and others.

Life is a miracle and death is the end. The path in between is so important, it's an infinite amount of moments that only moves forward in time. From the moment you come into the world until your last breath you have a huge responsibility- to make sure life was worth it.

August 16th

Happiness will not be achieved through relentless consumption. Are the peaceful Tibetan monks busy with orders from Amazon? You'll never get enough to make you truly happy. Happiness is a way of looking at things, it's appreciation, gratitude, peace and serenity in the present moment. The money you don't have won't bring you happiness through the products you don't need.

August 17th

Genesis, Chapter 1, Verse 27, "God created man in His own image, in the image of God created He him; male and female created He them."

Whether or not you believe in God you must admit that life is a miracle. Life is hardly possible when we really explore the topic. Imagine what the probability was that a star in the Milky Way Galaxy settled in a place that was a perfect distance from the sun, perfect enough to create life. This star tipped on its side and produced seasons. Its Moon is also the perfect distance to create tides. The conditions are more than perfect. Can it be a coincidence? Is it all predestined? In each and every one of us the divine particle exists.

According to the verse above every one of us is a God living on the earth. As such you have the ability and right to distinguish between good and evil. Every one of us is given the ability to create. You can create your life. It won't always be easy, but it will always be possible. Shortcuts don't allow for growth and appreciation. You must see your success through to the end. See how hard athletes train to get the results they want. This is the work ethic you need to achieve what you want. Create your life with the understanding that the divine particle resides in you. If you don't create your life someone else will do it for you and that won't allow you to realize your potential.

Take a deep breath and know that you have full control over your life and your decisions. Decide to be the creator of your life.

August 18th

Different but equal.

Tension and harmony exist at the same time. We're unique and special, there's no one like us in the whole world. Therefore, we all have to be different in some way and this difference can be perceived as threatening by some people. We're classified by sex, skin color, eye shape, geographical location, etc. The variety is beautiful, yet it threatens others who become hateful out of ignorance and fear.

Despite our differences we're actually very similar. We have similar fears, hopes, and dreams. We're all human beings so we should conduct ourselves as equals.

Remember that you're special, but among equals!

August 19th

A few years ago I read an article about billionaire Arcadi Gaydamak. The reporter asked him how he made his fortune. He answered the question with a question of his own, what had the reporter done that morning? The reporter replied that he had made himself coffee, read the morning papers and prepared himself for another day of work. The billionaire said that when he got up that morning he went straight into thinking about where he would get his next million.

The purpose of this example is to illustrate how the power of thought and focus creates reality. It requires training and awareness but hey, it's something we can all bring into our lives. Do we get up in the morning with creative joy and a clear vision? Or do we allow our thoughts to wander aimlessly, preoccupied with the small things, just trying to get through the day safely, but exhausted? This isn't a life of joy, therefore, we direct our thoughts and towards our vision. This will allow us to grow and develop our potential.

August 20th

Is there life after death?

This question has intrigued humanity from its first moments of consciousness. I don't know a person who returned to tell the tale however. Do you? While there are plenty of stories, if we rely on science there's no such proof, even if as conscious human beings we'd be happy to know that we continue on after we die. Lucky for us, there is life before death. But, think about how many people simply exist instead of actually living? Some people get up in the morning just because they didn't die at night. There's a huge difference between mere existence and living. Life is a miracle, something we must cherish every morning. Life is about compassion, love, kindness and gratitude.

Here is a little anecdote: someone has ascended to heaven. While waiting in line he sees two gates in front of him, one to Heaven and one to Hell. When he reached the end of the line he met an angel who instructed him to walk to the gates of hell. Surprised, he asked the angel, 'Why? After all I've been through? I made sure to do many good deeds from the little to the big, I made sure to respect God and live according to his ways! I have worked so tirelessly to be a good person that I've barely rested! I never took a vacation or owned a decent car. I gave all my money to the church!"

The angel answered that the only thing they looked at was whether someone had lived or whether they wasted the life they were given. Then, the Angel pointed once again to the gates of Hell.

August 21ᵗʰ

You probably got up this morning, looked out the window, and saw a ray or two of sun shining in. The sunshine every morning signals new opportunities. It's a new day with new beginnings. Practice waking up with positive energy. Don't look for positive energy outside of yourself, it exists within you. We can notice positive energy by practicing listening to ourselves. It exists within us and we are reminded of this by our bursts of creativity, enthusiasm and curiosity.

How can we nourish our bodies with that powerful life energy? First, remember that our body responds to our actions quickly. The well-known phrase of Hippocrates, "Let food be thy medicine and medicine be thy food" is a good example. To do this we must eat healthy foods like green vegetables, seeds and nuts, and replace the soft drinks with water. We need to take deep breaths, relax, and slow down. Don't forget to take responsibility because when you do, the excuses and justifications end.

Assure yourself that you'll fill yourself with goodness and let the positive energy flow in and out of you.

August 22th

Perseverance is the name of the game.

It's difficult, but extraordinarily rewarding. In the film, *All the Money in the World* the protagonist John Paul Getty, the richest man in the world, expressed that it's not difficult to become a billionaire but it's difficult to maintain that status.

The perfect example of this is in weight loss programs. Reaching our target weight is not difficult, but maintaining it is. We must keep on persevering to keep our victory. Another example is when a bird reaches the height that it wants to fly at it still has to persevere by continuing to flap its wings to maintain their height, otherwise they will start descending. Like the birds we need to keep flapping our wings once we reach our goal. Then the real journey begins: maintaining our achievements.

Even if you have reached your destination or goal, keep flapping your wings!

August 23th

What makes you grow?

Is it your light and serenity or your pain and scarcity during times of survival and fear? Of course, we grow during periods of survival, but most of the time after the suffering disappears we go back to the old habits.

My wife's uncle underwent bypass surgery. When we visited him at the hospital he said he had come to the realization that the life that had been given to him was a gift. Enthusiastically he told us how he intended to change his lifestyle. He wanted to reduce his workload, relax and spend more time with family. After sometime, when he returned home, it seemed that his lifestyle had indeed changed for the better, but slowly he returned to his previous ways.

What is your source of your growth and development? Is it due to a feeling of scarcity or is it due to the emergence of being and the desire to fulfill your potential as a human being? We can change without suffering and without being in a place of survival.

August 24th

What do we really want? Why do we get offended? Why do we feel alone when we are with other people? Why are we afraid of looking ridiculous and why are so many people afraid to speak in front of an audience?

Ultimately, we want to feel loved and to be seen. Everyone wants to be visible. It's natural and starts from infancy, but we must learn to disengage from that destructive external dependence and trust ourselves, love ourselves unconditionally and realize that we are all human with our nuances and uniqueness. This gives us freedom from dependence and allows us to fulfill ourselves.

Trust yourself and love yourself, and though not everyone will love you, agree with you or suffer for you remember: so what!

August 25th

Sometimes we just have to trust the path.

It isn't mere coincidence that it takes us somewhere. It leads us through the hidden path of our hearts. Our hearts are the authentic part of us that cannot be faked. It isn't by chance that you are rejected by certain jobs or that you get into a relationship with someone who treats you poorly. Eventually, we'll have to dive in and bravely explore why we repeatedly make the same mistakes and consistently expect different results. What is our hidden motivation? Do we really have the desire to always be blaming others and making excuses for ourselves? Is being immature going to be our choice?

The answer is within you, dive boldly.

August 26th

We are constantly being encouraged to multitask.
While we think we can run around completing everything at once, the truth is that our minds are working serially like computers. Our brains process information so quickly that it seems as if several tasks are being done simultaneously. By nature we're meant to do things sequentially, not concurrently. We can't hold a cup of coffee in one hand and drink it while writing with the other hand. We'd have to interrupt at least one of the two tasks to do the other. Our mind is built to perform task after task and think thought after thought, so we must seek out thoughts that are positive and constructive. This allows us to become happier because we have a foundation of positivity. This is how we practice optimism, joy, love and health. Negative thoughts reduce us and harm our health to the point of making us physically ill. Frustration and despair creep in. You are responsible for how you are physically affected by your environment. If you are stressed all the time or overworked it is your responsibility to change that.

Change your thoughts and change your attitude, you'll immediately experience a change in your mental health and energy. Do it now. There's no time like the present to bring change into your life!

August 27th

Anger, nervousness, frustration, disappointment; these are the emotions which fear hides behind.

Our fear of not being noticed, being unworthy, losing control, loss and fear itself resides deep inside us and hides behind different facades. Once we realize this it will be easier for us to see the fear in those close to us. Beneath the sadness, anger or frustration lies fear, the fear of not being seen, of not being important enough, of not being respected. We create our own reality so let's stop being angry and defensive and directly speak to our fears.

Once you do this you will see an instant change.

August 28th

There must have been a time in your life where you found yourself somewhere and wondered what the heck you were doing there.

You wondered when it would be over so you could finally get away from all these people and go back to the peace of your home. Even if you were supposed to be celebrating you felt loneliness and insecurity. It's a feeling that you have embraced and fostered with negative beliefs and this feeling is the source of the depression you cannot shake.

If you're already there and are imprisoned, challenge yourself. Confront this unhappiness as though it were a game. Play this game well. Roll the dice and change your attitude. Make a firm decision to enjoy the maneuvering of your emotions to a better place. After all, you've been playing the game every day without knowing it, so why not choose to win and be happy now that you know how? The choices to be made regarding your feelings are yours and yours alone.

You determine how to feel. Pat yourself on the back and decide that you're going to enjoy everything. What is there to lose with this approach? Your suffering.

August 29th

Do you know when we have the most fun?

When we feel whole, safe, loved. Those feelings don't come from external sources. As adults the best way to attain freedom and mental well-being is to be comfortable with ourselves. We must understand what our needs are and where our true desires come from. We need to allow ourselves to experience passion and dream of the unattainable. You must dedicate your life to achieving these things.

Most people unconsciously live the desires and dreams of others. They become the background character before they notice that something is wrong. When a child completes a milestone the parent's satisfaction with it does not reach the exhausted child, who has already been given a new goal to complete. The child becomes empty while the parents are satiated. Living the dreams of others brings no satisfaction.

A few of my friends have made the transition from working at a "respectable" place with a lucrative salary to careers that border on the abstract or nonconformist. They are jobs that they dreamt of as children, but were swayed by other people when they became adults. One friend, who worked with me in investment management, is now a talented oil painter with gallery shows across the country. The path that leads to happiness sometimes seems strange, but the content person walks their path cheerfully and that's what matters. What's important is whether the path you take is yours. Don't follow the breadcrumbs left by someone else or be pushed along by well-wishers who think they know what you need. Choose the path that brings you closer to your own dreams and desires. It's your path, walk proudly.

August 30th

If there's anything that never stops its time.

Time constantly moves and pushes us forward. We all move with it and watch life move with it too. We know when a baby should start turning over, when its first words are due, when they'll be toilet trained and when they'll start school. We know more or less about when we're expected to return the bodies God lent us and move to the great unknown.

Life is a journey that doesn't really end so we shouldn't get stuck on a moment. Some moments are so chaotic to us with our anger, our wrong words, erupting rage and sense of doom that follows after we lose control. But, life is a journey. Be forgiving with yourself and others. Everyone wants to go through this journey with as few upheavals as possible. Everyone is looking for happiness.

If a moment is too hard to handle, remember that there's still a lifetime of moments ahead.

August 31th

Today I will share my thoughts.

We sometimes encounter discomfort and it's wise to accept it. This is expressed through patience and by finding ways to bear the discomfort without losing stability or the ability to take action.

But what about the ego that wants to win at all costs even if it means destroying our body? I have learned that accepting myself will weaken the ego's power. I remind myself that everything is fine and that there's no room for self-doubt or pointless disapproval.

"Everything is relative," Einstein said. "Often we judge ourselves according to others, which is where the seeds of dissatisfaction are sown." There will always be someone richer and more successful. Remind yourself not to compare yourself to others in order to avoid burning jealousy, self-hatred and feelings of failure. Compare yourself to only yourself and changes in compassion, love and self-acceptance will occur. This way we can go with the flow in terms of aspirations, achievements and listening internally for what is right for us.

September

September 1st

Practice being creative, positive, loving, enthusiastic and happy.

It might sound like a cliché, but words have power and that power changes our experiences. Experiences change our actions and that changes our reality. I started with the word "practice" because the only way to achieve permanent change is through constant practice. Practice ultimately leads to perfection.

However, sometimes we practice something in the wrong way and end up creating bad habits. This diminishes the good effects of practice and creates self-doubt and enslavement, even fear. For example, if you keep telling yourself that you are bad at math, eventually you will be bad at math because you've practiced telling yourself that to perfection!

During practice sessions we tend to judge ourselves harshly. This habit creates frustration and depression. We must pay attention to how we practice. We must not be overly-critical of ourselves or others. When we do this we are essentially practicing making ourselves and others unhappy. This repetition eventually creates negative thoughts and behaviors. So, if we're going to constantly practice, then why not practice growth and become a better person?

September 2nd

The best way to help others is by taking the responsibility of managing your feelings.

It isn't uncommon to find out that our friends or relatives sometimes feel depressed too. It's not our job to change how they feel. Burdening ourselves with the responsibility of another person's emotions has too great a cost. It's too much to take on the guilt of another person's depression. Many people fail to separate themselves from another person's sadness and then they spiral themselves. Depression is contagious and we may even lose our kindness and compassion due to the frustration of trying to change another person's feelings and failing.

Remember that it isn't your job to make others happy. First and foremost, take care of yourself and make sure you have a balanced life. If we are aware of our emotions and empower ourselves through positive thought and action, then we will be an inspiration to others and can provide a supportive and stable shoulder to our loved ones.

Be understanding, compassionate, empathetic and listen with love. Hug, love and smile, that is our endeavor for today!

September 3rd

We aren't able to change how others see us.

There will always be those whose opinion of us is negative and there will always be those who appreciate you. Some will look for the good in you and others will judge you harshly. If you keep practicing positive thinking the destructive opinion of others will be silenced. Therefore, you must concentrate on the good in you and your uniqueness. Cultivate love for yourself and soon no opinion will matter but your own. Remember that the thoughts of others create their realities, not yours. Use positive thinking to create a reality you deserve.

Thoughts of hatred, envy, and negativity from others won't be able to overcome the love you have for yourself.

September 4th

This is the golden age of plastic surgeons, diet gurus and personal trainers for success in life. All of that is happening because you're human and for a long time just being human hasn't been enough. Endless commercials, television programs and interviews with experts in different fields constantly advising us how to become perfect. Our body is limp, our stomachs not flat enough, our breasts are sagging and the butt too. The psychologists continue to invent various strange diseases and the magic pills that solve them. Plastic surgeons promise to bring us closer to society's model of perfection and as a result you should be happier. Older actors already seem expressionless from all the Botox injections. The race to perfection never ends, it's elusive, a grand ideal that is not achievable. Shouldn't we stop and check to see if we're doing the right thing? We must remember that we're human, so we aren't perfect and that's alright. We must learn to accept ourselves as a whole; accept our behaviors, thought patterns and how we look. So let's complete the simple task of forgiving ourselves for our "disadvantages"!

Accept yourself and come to terms with your imperfections because you're human. Leave the perfection to Photoshop and other software programs because what you see in the media is just an illusion and you must not allow yourself to be lost in a dream world. Plant your feet in reality and carry on!

September 5th

Learn to say THANK YOU.

I don't mean the thank you that you'd say to a salesperson, or to someone who is holding the door or elevator for you. That's an automatic and thoughtless thank you. It's a social behavior, a mannerism, a habit. It's not wrong, of course, it's always nice to hear.

But there's a much bigger spiritual thank you that must be said more often. There should be divine gratitude for obvious things that aren't so simple. Say thank you to your creator no matter what you call them. The miracle of life should never be taken for granted, nor health, family or friends. For better or worse they're with you and you must be grateful for that. If you have a roof over your head you're lucky since there are many places where a roof isn't provided. Say your spiritual thank you's each day. There are many who are hungry, who are refugees that are disaster-stricken, war-weary, or who knows what else. Learn to say thank you because you are alive!

September 6th

The greatest inventors of our time didn't follow the crowd and didn't listen to others who told them they wouldn't succeed. How many of you would have given up, unlike Thomas Edison, the inventor of the light bulb? How many experiments would it have taken you to give up? The incandescent lamp was invented after 2,000+ experiments failed. What made Mr. Edison stick it out: a bit of stubbornness spiced with self-esteem, a pinch of self-discipline over a hot bowl of confidence and a big glass of desire for a breakthrough.

The course these famous inventors chose wasn't normal for their time. Thomas Edison was a pioneer and to be one you had to think differently. How? They were illogical! So let's be illogical. Let's think of a nontraditional solution to a problem.

Is it logical that the universe is finite? Or would it be more correct to say that the universe is infinite? And what about time? Is there something out there that came first with nothing coming before it? Does that make sense? Logic can be the most illogical thing. Logic is a matter of perception after all, just like there are some who say that it's illogical for God to exist while others sacrifice their lives for God because they *know* he's real.

So, let's be illogical and achieve some groundbreaking results.

Think of a problem or an obstacle you've come across in your life and think of a new, refreshing and creative way to master it. Plant another seed in your garden... be illogical!

September 7th

Focus on one thing at a time and do it well. I write this from personal experience.

I've always made to-do lists for the tasks that I wanted completed. But, not so long ago my main task had always been to finish my to-do list, no matter the quality of the work. The task itself was not what I focused on, it was checking it off the list. The goal was completely missed since the tasks needed to be done in a focused and careful manner, but I was captivated by just finishing as fast as possible.

Slowly I came to the conclusion that the goal should be to focus on one thing at a time, do it the best I could and only then move on to the next task. The amount of tasks I wrote down each day had also been significantly reduced. I'm no longer in a race against the clock. The tasks are performed in a satisfactory manner. I am able to handle things professionally and correctly since it's not rushed. It has made a difference in my life and there's no reason why it shouldn't.

September 8th

Just do it.

As simple or difficult as it is.

Many times, we get stuck and walk in place moving neither forward nor backward. We tell ourselves that if we try harder, take more risks or dare more, we'd achieve what we want. In fact, what often stops us are our thoughts that are mixed with fear, doubt and lack of faith in ourselves. These thoughts hold us back.

Sometimes all we need to do is silence those thoughts and simply act.

So today find something you want. Stop thinking about it and act on it.

At worst you could succeed!

September 9th

The classroom of life; from the moment we come into the world we begin learning. At first, we learn the basic things: how to communicate by crying, laughing and smiling. We learn about the world through our parents. We take our first steps and learn how to walk despite falling countless times. We never had parents who whispered in our ears "Don't waste your efforts, you won't succeed." On the contrary, we were encouraged to stand up again and again and continue trying. Our parents believed in us. We fell because we weren't ready to walk yet. Determination exists in us and accompanies us our whole lives. We simply forget we have it. Determination is what helps us get up again even though we fall and fail endless times.

Today we also fall but we often stay down. What has changed? Our belief, that's what changed. Instead of treating the fall as a failure and giving up and letting a feeling of inferiority lead, we must instead create a habit of asking ourselves, "What can I learn from this? What can I learn about myself, my values, my perception?" We should understand that it isn't a failure but part of the learning process.

September 10th

It's only a hyphen.

—

That's it.

—

A hyphen.

A hyphen that you place between two dates to keep them separate. The date of birth and the date of death are apart, different and separate. Usually, a sentence or two is written on the tombstone and that's it. That's what a whole life comes down to. It isn't sad, it's just a fact. It also means that we are given the responsibility to live life well. It's our soul's responsibility to make sure that the hyphen between our two dates will be something we can be proud of, something valuable and meaningful to us. The time the hyphen represents must be important, well used and complete because this is our life and we will walk this path only once so we should make it worth it. The road should be worth walking and the choices we make along the way should be ours. We should look back one day on our journey and the choices we made and say it was worth it!

Make it worth it *for you,* and make every moment count.

September 11ᵗʰ

Good books are written all the time and on every subject in the world.

Books have the tremendous power to teach us and help us grow. I read books all the time on topics that interest me and help me become a better person. When I look back, I cherish the path that I took and I see my development. I've found that books helped me to gain knowledge, insights and understanding on many different subjects. I make sure to read a book every night and I always have a pile of books next to me. This habit allows me to become smarter, more peaceful, more self-controlled and in short, more of everything. More than what I am now.

I want to share a small list of books that I found very interesting. Remember that there will always be another book that pops up and is more up to date or more relevant. But still, below is a list that I believe is a must-read regarding personal growth.

Books for personal growth:
- *Your Erroneous Zones* by Dr. Wayne Dyer
- *Creating Miracles in Everyday Life* by Dr. Wayne Dyer
- *Emotional Freedom* by Dr. Judith Orloff
- *Conversations with God* by Neil Donland Walsh
- *The Power of the Subconscious* by Joseph Murphy
- *Man's Search for Meaning* by Victor Frenkel

Books on nutrition:
- *The New Optimum Nutrition Bible* by Patrick Holford

Books on economics:
- *The Intelligent Investor* by Benjamin Graham
- *Think and Grow Rich* by Napoleon Hill

Books on improving personal skills:
- *How to Win Friends and Influence People* by Dale Carnegie
- *Men Are from Mars, Women Are from Venus* by Dr. John Gray
- *The Power of Touch* by Phyllis K. Davis
- *Breaking The Limits* by Alon Ullman

Books on time management:
- *Eat That Frog* by Brian Tracy
- *In Praise of the Slowness* by Carl Honore

Books that transform:
- *The Secret* by Rhonda Byrne
- *Creating Reality* by Esther Hicks

This is a partial list, but these books have certainly allowed me to grow and become a better person towards myself and others.

September 12th

Make it a habit to brush your teeth as early as possible.
There are many benefits to brushing your teeth in terms of health, but beyond that it's an agreement with yourself to finish eating for the night. Consumer culture has taught us to end the day in front of a screen with various snacks. We don't need research to tell us that consuming fats, sugar, salt and chemicals before sleep is harmful. The last thing our digestive system needs after working all day is to work while you sleep.

Make the habit, as I did, to brush your teeth at least 3 hours before you go to bed. At first it will be a bit strange and difficult, but over time it will become second nature. Like any new habit, start gently. Brush your teeth a bit earlier each night and after a short while the gap will increase to a few hours.

Start today! You'll benefit from a guaranteed deep sleep and a decrease in side effects like late-night heartburn. It works. I promise.

September 13th

Power!

The lust for it motivates us both positively and negatively. For many, the pursuit of power is the main goal. It's often hidden behind other names like respect, pride or a position title such as CEO, president, etc. People are willing to do anything to achieve it.

The Roman philosopher, Seneca, defined absolute power as self-control! Aim and aspire for that and you'll eventually connect to the source of inexhaustible power, the power that lies within you.

I want to share a tragic story with you. It's about Dudu Topaz who was a very famous entertainer. Everyone knew him. He starred in movies, made art and hosted a talk show. His program was so successful. On Fridays my family and I would sit around the TV screen and enjoy an evening filled with fun entertainment. He earned the title The King of Ratings. He enjoyed the power that came from the recognition of his work. Slowly, however, his fame began to fade and its radiance waned. Since his source of power was external, he began to feel an unbearable loneliness. Eventually his anger took over and he decided to take revenge on the media's leaders by sending people to beat them up. There was also suspicion that he was trying to hurt other prominent actors and entertainment people out of jealousy from their success. His end was bitter. He committed suicide in his jail cell.

See how external forces produce severe dependence? True power resides within us. We deserve to enjoy the spiritual and physical abundance that exists in the universe. When we rely on inner strength there's nothing in the world that can stop us and we don't need recognition from others for our own existence!

Trust yourself and look inside where the real power lies!

September 14th

There are universal laws that supersede time and culture.

It was when Hillel the Elder, the last president of the San-hedrin, was asked to teach a man the entire Torah quickly that he replied, "What you hate, don't do to your friend. This is the whole Torah, and the rest is how to learn to do that." The sixth commandment in the Tablets of the Covenant says, "Thou shalt not kill" a rule of great importance, is based on the rule "What you hate, don't do to your friend. This is the whole Torah!" This rule is also positively worded as, "Love thy neighbor as thyself." This rule can have two interpretations. The first is to love others as you love yourself. The second interpretation is to look at ourselves, right at the evil that we have within and love it since it is a part of us. There's no good without evil, otherwise how do we know what's good?

Follow these rules consciously. You'll invite abundance and love into your life as you transform yourself and the way you see the world.

September 15th

We know everything.

We have already heard everything and like they say "There is nothing new under the sun." We have already encountered everything and yet there's a difference between knowing something and taking action with our knowledge!

I remember during one of the personal empowerment workshops that I attended the teacher said that we have already heard this entire workshop somewhere else. He had nothing new to tell us, yet here we are. It's like a heavy smoker who has all the information they need to improve their health. They know that smoking is harmful, that the chances of lung cancer is high, that their vocal cords are deteriorating, and that their chronic cough and shortness of breath come from their heavy smoking. They know all this, but it doesn't matter!

One of the strongest forces that exists within us is our will power. Sometimes it comes too late for smokers, but that's fairly common. The secret is to take responsibility now! Don't wait for the inevitable encounter with disaster to change. Those who participated in the personal empowerment workshop did so out of conscious choice to grow and improve. Most of them have probably already heard what was taught in the class, but they went anyway to listen, take responsibility, change themselves and their environments.

The information is within you too. Decide to use it for your growth and to fulfil the tremendous potential within you. Take responsibility now!

September 16th

Where are you now and where do you want to be?

This gap stems from your thoughts, the same endless stream of thoughts that flows all the time. You need to be aware, flow with the current and gently direct it towards the direction you want. Remember that the current is powerful. Examine where it's going and direct it gently, with determination, perseverance and awareness. Remember that it all starts with a thought and that has the power to create the reality you desire. To do so you must take the reins.

The best time to do this is now!

September 17th

What kind of life are you living? Are you living a satisfactory life, excited about the future or are you living an unsatisfactory one thinking thoughts like, "If I had done X, if I had behaved differently, if I had taken different actions my life would have been much different." Such a life is an enslavement to suffering, an addiction to bitterness and constant living in the past while the present passes without meaning or purpose. Remember the prayer of peace written by Niebuhr in 1932, "Grant me the serenity to accept the things I cannot change, the courage to change the things I can, and the wisdom to know the difference."

You're a creature born of thoughts. Let go of the chains of the past or the present you're missing will join that list of failures. As with any addiction it's very difficult and you'll experience withdrawal, but then you will be able to focus your attention on the present moment and create abundance and happiness in your life.

Look forward, the past cannot be changed, but the future has not yet begun and is still in your hands.

September 18th

What will happen if we slowly peel away our protective layers? First, we would find that we have more energy because we are not hiding or pretending anymore. Second, we'll realize that fear was our primary driver for concealing our weaknesses and creating a false image of ourselves. All of that energy is now being freed up for our growth. Suddenly we'll feel light, we won't have to justify ourselves anymore. Humor and lightness will become a part of our lives and a lot of drama will disappear. You'll have the resources you need to really do what makes you happy, satisfied and fulfilled. You'll experience vitality, compassion and love. Every person is meant to be a sociable and allied creature. We'll stop letting our egos decide how we behave and we'll see the humor in life.

Do you not believe it? I know, I was skeptical too. Try doing what you care about, you'll succeed!

September 19th

The awareness between the pages of this book is connected in an intangible way. There is appreciation for our miraculous lives, acceptance of how things are, living in the present moment and gratefulness. It's a holistic vision, everything is intertwined with everything else.

I want to help you develop awareness about the food we give our bodies as well as our minds. Conscious eating is when we listen to our bodies. We should know the difference between eating out of hunger or when we're bored or emotional. We need to be aware of our water intake, the boring drink that our bodies crave. We need to be aware about basic, organic food and also what harms our bodies like excess sugar, salt, artificial sweeteners, preservatives and empty calories.

Make it a habit to choose simplicity. When you're thirsty, drink water. Coffee isn't necessary. A banana with some almonds will do a better job of getting you energized. Eat organic fruits and vegetables. You'll soon get used to the acquired taste and your body will thank you. You'll feel fresh and your skin will look better. When I switched to a healthier diet the warts on my toes and thumbs disappeared. Before, I would have to go to the doctor every few months to freeze them with nitrogen and that didn't really help. My stress levels are now low and I'm full of life that radiates from the inside out.

It's easier than you think. You just need to start with one small change. Once that change becomes a habit, move on to the next change. Our bodies will quickly adapt to the new changes and heal faster than before.

September 20th

The freedom to be you is your right.
It's fun to take off your mask, experience everything and live life to the fullest with love and joy, sorrows and pain. What fun it is to feel everything with our five senses. What a gift it is to cherish ourselves, the miracle that is us, since the chances of existing were zero to impossible. Here we are, so cherish, cherish and cherish again. Live life in its variety of colors. Yes, there'll be painful and sad moments but that's what makes us all actors on this stage of life.

September 21th

The fear of making mistakes is often an obstacle to self-fulfillment, success and a comfortable life.

We often got conflicting messages when we were young. We, as children, loved to experiment and explore the unknown. It seemed like nothing could stop us (except for the adults of course). Those who want the best for us prevent us from making mistakes. They said things like, "Don't climb because you can fall." "Don't run, it's dangerous." "Don't jump into the water." Don't, don't, don't and don't! There is no doubt that these rules may have kept us alive and prevented us from getting hurt, or from breaking our bones like our parents always promised we would. But, as adults, we carry this way of thinking into our present lives and it doesn't distinguish between real and imagined dangers. One of the dangers we encounter as adults is change. We live in a constantly changing environment and it's a natural part of life, but as children we are programmed to believe that change is dangerous. Change is inevitable, we can't hide from it or stay infinitely afraid. Change contains seeds of success and seeds of failure. What is failure if not just a different result that the one we wanted? We can learn from failure so it's never a waste of time.

Don't be afraid of making mistakes or failing. It's a natural part of life and is part of learning and growing. Remember that success cannot be learned. Failure is the lesson. Learn the lesson and try again. Everything's fine, you're still on the playing field. Don't expect yourself to score a basket every time, just keep trying!

September 22th

I once heard, "don't be a 'no' man, be a 'yes' man."
But everything should be in moderation. We live in a world where the desire to serve others and even put their needs above our own is considered noble. Over time we give up on our desires and take other's desires as our own. But the truth is strong, and it doesn't matter how deep we bury it, it will always come out. It will manifest itself as frustration, helplessness, impersonality and emptiness. The secret is balance, even the word "no" has benefits.

We must learn how to stand up for ourselves and say no! When it comes at the expense of our goals and happiness it is far too much to pay! Live your life because it's yours, only yours!

September 23th

Do you have enough?

You are probably thinking no. You're probably waiting for your next paycheck so you can buy what you need. But do you really need it? Don't fall for the advertisements or the constant brainwashing that happens around us every day.

You're probably addicted to consuming and you don't even know it. How will you fund what the advertisements show you what you need? Is it through overtime at work? Is that what you really want? Or is it just a trap? Wait a minute, there's an easier way, just take out a loan! Yes, it's simple, just don't forget that non-compliance that involves consequences to your finances with the banks and credit unions that provided it. And a small something else, but maybe not so important, the interest rate can be10 percent or more. Is it worth it?

You know the answer.

September 24th

Put the book down and look around you.

Are there people around you? If not, imagine that there are. They aren't really different from you. Genetically you're almost identical. The difference is much smaller than you think. Everyone is crossing the same track. Some of them are more successful and some of them less, but in the end everyone basically wants the same thing: to be seen, to be loved, to be appreciated and respected.

Sometimes we have the urge to shout, "Hey, I'm here!" Some people do this aggressively. Some people have a hammer and everything seems like a nail. Others caress and smile. Is your boss like that? Are your parents? They do their best and sometimes they don't know any better, just like you. They seek refuge and sometimes that refuge is easy to find. It can be in the form of addiction, anger, dissatisfaction, and toughness, but behind it all lies fear, the fear that they will not be seen! It isn't personal. That's just how your parents grew up and maybe because of them, you did too.

But, is there not more power in gratitude, refinement, quietness, and gratitude?

September 25th

Sometimes all it takes is one small step.

I'm not just talking about the big things. It could be as simple as a morning routine. A feeling of one small victory follows you throughout the day. I remember a speech by admiral William McRaven, where he warmly recommended starting the day by making the bed.

For me it takes a few seconds to make the bed and it's a task completed. What a way to start the day! The day seems lighter. As William McRaven said, "If you didn't have a good day, at least you come back to a made bed!"

September 26th

Find something or someone to look up to.

Sometimes we feel like we could have done better if we had acted differently. Someone we admired would have acted better.

I argue that life is a game and we're all pieces. Each one of us, according to our luck and choices, advances or stays still. Let's play the game and once in a while think about what we could have done, how the person we admire would have done it. Like an actor in a film, slip into your hero's costume and pretend to be them for a while. Do the things you believe they would. Let your admiration be your guide. This is a helpful and a good method to overcome obstacles.

I asked an actor friend of mine what he likes most about acting. He replied that he likes to explore different and weird characters and really live through them, experience their lives and enjoy different perspectives of life.

Life is a game, so let's play it!

September 27th

You're here *against all odds*. You owe the Universe your thanks.

As far as we know the earth is the only planet that fosters life in our universe. There are billions of suns. In order for lifeforms like us to form, the earth has to be just the right distance from the sun. If we had been slightly farther away the earth would have been nothing but a frozen star. If we were just a few miles closer we'd be a burning star. The inclination of the earth on its axis is what produces our seasons. The existence of our moon is what brings stability. It prevents large changes to the rotation of the earth which would lead to extreme and destructive weather conditions. And where did all this water come from? It wasn't here when the earth was a stew of basalt rocks and volcanic eruptions. And what's more... our water is in a liquid form. Of course, as the earth rotates and the core of the earth heats it produces a magnetic field that protects us from destructive solar radiation. Without this protection we wouldn't survive. All of these things worked out perfectly for us to support life.

Besides all that, the sperm that became you competed with hundreds of millions of others in the race to fertilize the egg. You're the one who managed to get there first and with great effort penetrated the ovary and eventually became a fetus. There are a trillion times more reasons why you shouldn't have been born and yet here you are! Isn't it a miracle to be grateful for all the time? Acknowledge that you're unique and special and as unusually lucky as the person who wins the lottery.

Cherish yourself, you're a jewel in the crown of creation.

September 28th

I have found that one of the most effective ways to be happier is to be of service to others.

It's already known that giving to others and volunteering contributes to our happiness. I find myself giving directions to a lost pedestrian, letting cars pass me, giving money to anyone who asks me on the street, and always smiling. I held the elevator door open for an older neighbor, volunteered to drive my daughter's girlfriends to a movie, etc. I discovered that it slowly became my nature, a kind of behavioral adaptation that made me see things in a positive light. Actions that used to make me angry now make me smile. If a car roars past me I see it as the other driver is in a bigger hurry than I am and I say to myself that it has nothing to do with me, it's nothing personal at all.

September 29th

"Without you, I'm half a man."

These are some of the lyrics I've been hearing lately. It's connected to the recurring theme in movies: the obsession of winning a lover to have happiness and end suffering. In reality, many suffer more from low self-esteem, insecurity and low self-worth than they do from living alone.

Some of us speak the sentences we believe in like, "I'm so stupid." "I'm ugly." "Once again I went out of my way and no one appreciated me." But when we see our loved ones showing signs of weakness or depression we immediately help with kind words, caressing touches, softness and helpful advice. Why not treat ourselves the same way? Why not get used to talking to ourselves softly, pleasantly, lovingly and in the same way we treat others? When we help ourselves, we're able to help others better.

Loving ourselves isn't a cliché, it should be a way of life. If you haven't already started, start now!

September 30th

Let's think for a moment about who you are.

"Well, I'm ..." and usually, by the second or third sentence of describing yourself you'll talk about your career. "I'm a waiter, a doctor, a student, a teacher, a lawyer" ... no no! This isn't what I asked. I asked who *you* are, what are *your* character traits, values, visions, dreams? "Oh no, I'm lazy, I produce little, I'll always be a coward." Wait a minute, that's not you! There's no reason for you to talk like that about yourself! You must understand, someone has programmed you to believe these things. Was it your father? Mother? A teacher? "My father always dreamed I'd be a doctor, but that was never what *I* wanted." Are you living other people's dreams? Are you really living your own life?

Start by asking yourself who you are, or rather who do you want to be? What are the values of those you look up to? What beliefs, hopes or dreams propel them forward? Think like your hero and see how quickly you'll become just like them.

October

October 1ˢᵗ

Worry is so common these days that our world seems full of danger.

Times have changed. Unlike in the past, a considerable number of the dangers we face today are intangible. In the past the dangers and worries were physical and touched on death. In the modern world, the worries are for the most part mental and have no outward physical effects. Over time the worry exhausts and depletes our energy. From there it's a short journey to the physical realm of disease, chronic fatigue or unhappiness.

Is all this really necessary? In most cases our concerns only exist in our wild dreams. Worry lives in the future, but has nothing to do with the present. It so happens that we aren't always present and quite often get lost in our own imagination. What's the point of worrying when it distracts us from the present moment and convinces us that the world isn't safe? Ultimately, most of the things that we're worried about never happen. The good news is that this is an acquired habit and as such, it can be changed.

Today, practice looking through the smoke screen and gloomy imaginings. Practice sowing positive thoughts and stop assuming the worst will happen because it usually only happens in your head. Breathe, trust yourself, believe that the good wins and remember that thoughts create reality!

October 2nd

A little bit about worry.

Sometimes we worry. It takes our time and corrupts our souls. It doesn't rest. Our mind creates dreadful scenarios. Fear is a self-perpetuating cycle that makes us afraid. It seems like we may have developed an addiction to being worried. If so, then this is the time to stop!

Being worried doesn't serve us, and sometimes we even use it as a way to control others. When we tell someone "Don't go abroad or I will be worried" we are guilting the other into doing or not doing something that we want. Worry disguises itself as caring, but it only helps us serve our unrealistic fears.

It's extremely rare that worrying helps resolve any conflict! Can you remember how many times you were worried last year and what it was about? Was that worry justified? I am sure that most situations were resolved and didn't turn out the way your fear imagined. Wasn't it a waste of time and mental/physical energy? Ultimately, the fearful scenes in your mind never came to life. Admit it.

Practice releasing worry from your heart and if, God forbid, something bad does actually happen remember that worry will *not* solve anything.

October 3rd

What are you really guilty of?

There are many aspects that hold us back from growing. One of them is guilt. Guilt has an amazing ability to weaken us and make us feel worthless. What is the source? The insecurity in our abilities and the feeling that we're inferior to others. Mistakes and failures are a natural part of our journey in life and they have an amazing ability to teach us lessons. We must internalize that everything is okay! So when you find yourself wallowing in feelings of guilt, understand that this event that happened can't be changed. The only thing that can be changed is your feeling about that event. Guilt is just sins of the past that are preventing us from acting in the present. So, we must become aware of what we are guilty about and then release it by fully accepting what happened. This is a new pattern of thinking where we accept that the past can't change, but our attitudes towards it can.

Today, be aware of situations where feelings of guilt creep up and sabotage your present. If you don't find it then you're in a great position, be thankful for that.

October 4th

Glass ceiling.

Most of us are familiar with this concept where the path to advancement has been blocked for some because of their gender, race, socio-economic status, etc. But the glass ceiling doesn't only exist in the workplace, it exists in the unconscious and in many aspects of our lives.

Where are your glass ceilings? If you look closely, you'll see that you have many. Is it in your unbearable perception of yourself? Why not smash the glass ceiling and find out that you really have no limits? Do you have a glass ceiling regarding your fitness? Why shatter too? These ceilings were placed by ourselves so we need to break them.

It's your responsibility to identify where your glass ceilings are and then shatter them.

October 5ᵗʰ

When tragedy strikes suddenly *everything* becomes smaller.
The annoyances that once ruined our day don't mean anything anymore. A tragedy allows us to be grateful for the little things that we do have and forget about the small inconveniences.

Value your life. It's OK to strive for more. It's natural, but don't become bitter working for more when you already have enough. You're on your way to your future, on your own path. The roads are long and sometimes difficult, but nevertheless remember to say thank you. Don't forget to thank yourself as well, you deserve it. You're part of the miracle of life. Always remember that!

Think of all the things that you take for granted. Go over the list and say thank you to those you overlook most often! The annoyances that ruined our day or the milk that spilled on the table this morning suddenly doesn't mean anything. A tragedy allows us to be grateful for the little things and forget about the small inconveniences.

October 6th

Today, we'll bring some compassion into our lives.

Sometimes we experience a coldness within ourselves. We're too strict and our threshold of expectation is unrealistic. It's only a matter of time before we fail. We can justify our self-condemnation by our lack of success. Are we really destined to live with the unrealistic objective of completing tasks and goals? Who puts this impassable obstacle in our way?

Modern life encourages us to be efficient and to get the best out of every situation. During our economic studies in college we worked vigorously and constantly thought about how we could be more efficient. The cause behind these thought patterns was derived from the "problem of scarcity." The existence of shortages requires streamlining and optimization at all times. But is this a desirable human behavior or will we eventually be doomed to retire exhausted from the race?

Focus on the fact that you're a human and not a machine.

We're in an age of material and spiritual abundance. Notice the immense wealth held by certain individuals. Look at the amount of food thrown out on one side of the world while the other side is on the brink of starvation. Scarcity is not the problem, but the way materials and food are divided across the globe is.

Slow down. Show compassion and sensitivity towards yourself and learn to accept that despite what you have or don't, you're okay. You are human and you shouldn't expect to be perfect.

Take care of yourself. You deserve it. Forgive yourself. Start now!

October 7th

What would have happened if you weren't wrong?

You probably would have followed a different, safer path, without bumps or dangers. But is this path really the right one for you? It's boring without challenges that help us grow. We learn from our mistakes when we accept that we'll make mistakes. The only one who doesn't evolve is the one who does nothing and never risks anything. What a terrible way to live!

The biggest mistake is to live like that without mistakes or new experiences. Remember that people regret the things they didn't do rather than the things they did!

Don't be afraid to make a mistake, this is life!

October 8th

"Don't worry, be happy."

This is the chorus from Bobby McPherson's famous song. The source of lyrics comes from Maher Baba, an Indian Guru.

These words have immortal power and must be engraved into our souls.

Neither the situation we're in, nor the circumstances are relevant to be happy. We are solely responsible for our happiness and our happiness is determined by our thoughts and feelings.

Happiness doesn't depend on external factors. Happiness doesn't depend on our environment. We must act and practice happiness. We must internalize the fact that we are solely responsible for our destiny and happiness. Let's practice this and practice not worrying. Let's try to be happy each and every moment.

Like every habit it takes time to worry less, but the reward will be immense.

When worry takes over, sing Maher Baba's song. Let happiness replace your worry. You deserve it.

October 9th

Everything is fine

"Everything is fine." These words have greater weight than their syntactic meaning. This is a worldview that I invite your heart to embrace. I have long since adopted these words which have empowered me time after time. You must recognize that life has its own course. It isn't personal, it's natural and "everything is fine." Things happen whether we like it or not and our way of accepting it is understanding that everything is fine. Even if it isn't really fine for us, it is.

"Everything is fine" contains the basic understanding that we have little control over circumstances and events in our life. Sometimes we're mistaken and think "this is wrong" and immediately become victims of the circumstance. No! Remember everything is fine!

As a human we'll continue to encounter unpleasant situations throughout our lives, situations in which we are ready to give up everything to avoid it. Life is stronger than we are and all that is left for us to do is internalize, embrace and say to ourselves, "Everything is fine."

Today, be aware of situations where you feel uncomfortable, stressed or under pressure and say to yourself, "Hey, everything is fine!"

October 10th

Everything is possible. This insight can help in situations and interactions where we feel trapped, afraid or when we've reached a dead end. But it's at that moment when it's most important to remember that everything is possible. It's true that you must try and fail, but never fail to try just because you think it can't be done. We are sometimes told that something may be impossible. In fact, they might be right! But always remember that just because it's impossible for them, it in no way proves that it will be impossible for you.

The next time you come across a situation where people tell you something is impossible, look at them compassionately and remember that while it may be true for them, it doesn't mean it's true for you. Remember you make all the decisions in your day-to-day life. Why not decide that everything is possible instead of even considering you might not do it right? Choose to try the impossible. Maybe you'll even surprise yourself!

October 11th

There's someone who thinks they can and someone who thinks they can't. They are both right. Which one do you want to be?

You are right no matter which you choose. Why? Because that's what you've decided. This is most important when you decide whether you can succeed or not, and you'll always be right. Over 100 billion people have already lived and every one of them was right about whether they could do something or not. There's nothing new under the sun so if others before you have done something there's no reason you can't too. But you may be a pessimist who will of course consider objective limitations. To be real, However, there's no act that has not been done before you by millions of people millions of times. Anything is possible and ultimately, if you think you can or if you think you can't you will be right.

So I'll repeat, which one do you want to be?

October 12th

Exercise must be part of your daily routine.

You don't have to prepare for the Olympics, but your body will thank you for even the smallest amount of attention. Even if you don't feel like it, even if there are more important *things* to do, find a few minutes each day to perform a physical activity. There are 1440 minutes in a day and if you spend fifteen minutes exercising it's only 1% of your day.

Get up! Stretch, go for a walk or do any other activity. Do it without complaining. Give your body one percent of the day!

October 13th

What is your purpose in life?

Money? Power, strength, health, abundance, to make the world a better place? What is your purpose? What do all these things have in common? The goal of happiness.

That's it.

Happiness, as we've discovered, is a learned process. We need positive thoughts daily, hourly and by the second. Even though we all have a desire to be happy there is a right and wrong way to do it. You need to really think about what matters to you and what makes you feel happy, peaceful, and calm. Smile, relax and take responsibility for your thoughts. The way your body reacts is not completely under your control, however, you can control how you react to circumstances.

October 14th

Remember that not everything is perfect.

The world doesn't dance to the music of our flutes. There are a lot of gray areas, not everything is black and white. The roller coaster of life is a scary journey into the unknown. Control is never really in our hands although we sometimes believe we are likened to gods. We are just human, stardust, here for a short time, destined to float through life trying to be happy.

Remember, everything is fine. This is your life. Failures and successes are just chapters in your book of life. Live your life to the fullest and remember that everything can be as you desire. No one else can write your story for you.

October 15th

"Cast thy bread upon the waters: for thou shalt find it after many days."

These wise words came from King Solomon. Casting bread or sowing seeds in water seems to be a futile exercise, but you don't know what the actual results will be. Solomon says, "In faith be generous, and in faith expect a return." Its ancient wisdom, thousands of years old, so obvious and yet sometimes so difficult to apply in life. Our egos scream not to be taken advantage of and to not seem frail.

Someone who acts with this adage in mind is a giver. They are someone who isn't afraid of sharing their ideas and material items or their kindness, compassion and generosity with others. They do not act in order to receive rewards. Studies have shown that volunteering, giving in its most basic form, can positively contribute to happiness.

We need to be willing to put ourselves out there and devote ourselves to others or causes that we believe in. We shouldn't be afraid to be givers. When we give we also receive and when we don't give our energy is low. It's unfair to hold ourselves back by being unkind.

Release your fears and doubts. Practice giving and loving. Cast your bread upon the waters and be content that in time your generosity will be returned.

October 16ᵗʰ

I attended a memorial service for a friend of mine who passed away in 2013.

He was 39 when he died. Friends and family gathered around his grave. A sermon called Kaddish Amen was delivered. His memory was revived, but the pain still remains. My friend's niece gave a heartfelt speech where she said that when her beloved uncle passed away. She was only twelve years old. Today she is seventeen years old and understands the meaning of death and its accompanying pain and longing to have that person in your life again. Her uncle would remain thirty-nine forever. We'd continue to grow and change, but inevitably we are all going to lie in a grave like his one day. She'd noticed that the age of the dead never changed, it was only the living who marked the passing of time.

The day of my friend's passing was his first day of eternity. Standing by his grave showing our respect year after year, we knew that in time the moment will come when no one is left to pay respects. I had to smile. I don't recall this with sadness, on the contrary, it's a hunger for life that our dead ones mean to leave behind. Death reminds us to live life intensely, experience everything, love, hurt, try and fail, be brave, not give up on ourselves and to eat life hungrily because one day it will end no matter who you are. Before we close our eyes for our final sleep, let's say hey, it was worth it, it was wonderful and now it's done.

Carry on loved ones, carry on!

October 17th

Get used to thinking big.

This cliché is good advice. Most of our thoughts are similar ones that we thought the day before and the day before that. We waste our thoughts day after day on autopilot. Taking responsibility for our thoughts requires a lot of practice, but the reward is huge. Our thoughts precede reality so a change in thought will lead to a change in reality.

I invite you to think about the next big thing you want in your life. Let's plan it! What challenges and fulfills you? What's the next brave step you need to take in order to improve your attitude and quality of life? Is it changing careers or housing? Is there a relationship in your life that's reaching a plateau? Think consciously and then unconsciously. Imagine the reality that you want and embrace the fear and doubt. Treat your emotions as distractions from the bigger picture. Control your thoughts because if you don't focus you'll think idle thoughts with no constructive purpose.

Practice being aware and thinking about the next big thing.

October 18ᵗʰ

Your path won't always be clear.

Tread carefully if you don't know where you are. This is your path, a path chosen just for you. It may not reveal your destiny, but trust it and walk on even if you sometimes feel detached or confused. Trust me, this path was meant for you and when you walk it believe that it is right for you. Despite the disappointments, fears and doubts know that this is your path. Dedicate yourself to it. Walk it proudly. Trust it because it is yours.

October 19th

How do you see yourself?

We're constantly bombarded with advertisements that presents "ideal beauty" and success that is actually an illusion. To be successful we must be slim, in shape, have luxury watches and clothing. We must behave one way and strive for this and that. Have we forgotten what we look like? Isn't the "ideal" dictated by advertisements? We're doomed to a life of misery and we'll continue to support this illusion for eternity.

Every day new perfumes and status symbols are launched. This isn't a bad thing for those who can afford it but there are many who are addicted to this pleasure at the cost of mental, financial and familial health. I remember seeing a picture on the Internet of a cat looking at himself in the mirror while a magnificent lion looks back. Why not see your own lion?

Disability never prevented Stephen Hawking from reaching greatness and becoming one of the most brilliant minds in history. Did Helen Keller's loss of sight, hearing and speech prevent her from becoming a writer and social activist? The potential we have is infinite. All we have to do is look inside and see our lion.

October 20th

"There's a man who succeeded in life" my wife said to me one night.

She was talking about a lawyer that we saw one evening at a restaurant. Indeed, he was tastefully dressed and radiating luxury. But over the years, as I got to know him, I learned that he was divorced, not interested in his children and was addicted to coffee. I remembered what my wife had told me as I listened to him drone on about his newest twenty year old girlfriend. Successful, sure, if that's what successful is. How easy it is for us to label a wealthy man complete or someone with a high paying job successful. But is it accurate? Are they really satisfied with their life? Why are we in the richest period in history yet with a steady increase in drug addiction, alcoholism and mental illnesses? We should probably redefine success. I would define success as the harmony I bring into my life and the serenity projected from me. There needs to be self-love, gratitude and understanding that everything is my own choice. Success radiates out and is contagious.

Project this new success out to the universe instead of following your old patterns of working too hard, impressing strangers and amassing wealth. It's not worth being considered successful if the effort only makes us miserable.

October 21th

The search for happiness often ends in disappointment.
We all want to feel good and are willing to do a lot to get that feeling. Some of us turn to drugs and others to therapists. Others combine the two or make radical changes in their lives. But the answer is right under our nose. Recent studies suggest that 20 minutes of daily exercise is enough to improve our moods. True, it requires perseverance, but what doesn't? The improvements in satisfaction, calmness and peace are immeasurable. So here is the recipe: Spend five minutes a day on stretching. Stiff muscles have tension that must be released, you can see that dogs and other animals do this instinctively. I actually learned this from my dog. Give yourself a few minutes a day and remember to smile even if at first it's fake. Sports, even if it is for a few minutes, has a positive effect on our moods. Devote a few minutes to meditation, introspection and quieting the mind. Sit with your eyes closed, breathe slowly and listen to your silence and breathing. The last thing is writing; write for 5 minutes without stopping and without censorship. Let your creativity run wild.

Do it and over time you are guaranteed amazing results. Ah, and don't forget to be grateful!

October 22ᵗʰ

When you open your eyes in the morning you are wearing glasses.

Those glasses will determine what your day will look like. Will you choose the pink glasses to make your day brighter?

Today doesn't know what it is, if it's good or bad; it's all your interpretation. So what glasses are you going to choose to wear? It's in your power to shape the day so shape it well.

Every morning, with awareness, choose to wear the pink glasses. Do it with self-love and complete faith that this is your day to create.

October 23th

We live our life through our five senses, although some would say six.

The amount of input is endless. Every moment several senses come together to make up our reality. It's a subjective reality, an interpretation really. You could be at a restaurant and watch how a customer eats oysters with pleasure while you feel disgusted. What's different between the customer and yourself? Why are they enjoying it and you aren't? It's because of your interpretation, your set of beliefs, values and cultural perceptions.

Events that happen aren't good or bad, it's our interpretation that determines it. Once you understand this you have tremendous power; nothing and no one can ever force you to feel a certain way. The power is in you, even if you haven't learned how to use it. So go and see reality from another angle.

October 24th

Is it important to you?

If so, then why are you giving up so quickly? It's normal to feel fear from rejection or a lack of faith, but you know that you deserve the best so if it's important to you, don't give up. Be unusual, invincible and irrational. See how miracles take place before your eyes.

Remember that day or night cannot be changed and you cannot move the sun or stars, but everything man-made is temporary. Laws and regulations are constantly changing. What seems hopeless, with enough perseverance and willpower, can be overcome. Very little cannot be changed. It's exhausting and it requires perseverance and determination. You'll have to deal with and meet your fears and doubts. Sometimes they'll win, but with awareness and perseverance you will be invincible.

The ending is worth it, so if it's important to you don't give up.

October 25th

Remember that everything has benefits and a price to pay.

The decision to not choose is a choice itself, and the benefit is not having to commit to something. But the price you pay for that often hurts because someone else will have control over your circumstances. Your comfort zone also comes with benefits because you don't have to risk anything and you don't have to change (and we know that change isn't an easy thing). But what is the price? A lack of growth, adequacy, and mental health.

Are you always right? If you are then the benefit is huge, your ego that wants to devour everything is satisfied. You gain an intoxicating sense of power. But, the price is unbearably high. Relationships are destroyed and the feeling of victory is slowly replaced by feelings of dull pain and anger. Is it worth it? Absolutely not! So, remember that everything you do has benefits and a price that you have to pay.

If we decide to take responsibility for our choices then the price we pay is lower and we can gain long term benefits. Choose wisely.

October 26ᵗʰ

What are you going to choose?

In every situation we always have the right to choose, whether it's blaming someone else for something or dealing with the situation, giving up and complaining or looking at it as an opportunity. It's easy to run away from responsibility. It's certainly addictive, but all we will feel is misery. Weakness consumes energy and then we are left exhausted. Lack of responsibility causes degeneration and puts your life in the hands of others, which won't be handled in the same way that you would have it.

So take responsibility and deal with all situations because this is real life. Look at everything as a life experience that has come to enrich you and help you discover your potential.

October 27th

Where do you live?

I don't mean which city or country. I mean, in which time? Are you in this moment or are you stuck in the past? Are you replaying a certain event in your mind where you're constantly recreating how you would've done things differently?

I remember listening to an interview with a successful businessman. The interviewer asked him about a deal that failed. It had appeared in the newspapers and was a hot topic for a while. The man replied that successful people don't live in the past. Wow, what power those words have. The energy we use for frustration and our pathetic attempts to construct different scenarios in our minds doesn't help us at all, and yet many choose to do just that.

Remember this business man's words; successful people don't live in the past. I'll add that happy people don't live in the past either. They all live in the present.

October 28th

Rabbi Masya ben (son of) Charash said, "Be the first to greet *every person*, and be the *tail* of *lions* rather than the *head* of *foxes*." Chapter 4, Mishna 20.

During certain periods of my life I preferred to be a head of foxes. It means that it's easier to stand out among people who are weaker than us. When I was in elementary school I chose weird friends in order to feel good about myself. I was the leader of the group, but I was still a fox, inferior to the lion. This environment wasn't a challenge. There was no growth or development. Since then, I have promised myself that whenever I have a choice I will choose to be the tail of lions. Tail or not, I always want to be a lion. This will allow me to continue to develop, grow and work my way up to the head.

I invite you to live consciously so that you can grow. Choose the tail.

October 29ᵗʰ

Which thoughts are limiting you? They are the ones who seem to be waiting for the right time to trip you up. But it's not done purposefully, in fact, someone very important who cares about you planted them.

This was at a time when your garden, your young mind, absorbed everything and set some beliefs in stone. "You're too short." "You're just like your father!" "You'll never succeed living where you do." The limiting thoughts continue, "There's no point in trying; it's too dangerous, too scary, impossible, or impractical. Why should I succeed when so many others fail? I don't have what it takes." I'm sure that if you check your inventory of limiting thoughts you'll find a few that I've mentioned among them. Even when you don't need to be chastised, those thoughts are there behind the scenes. But ask yourself, "Where do I want to be?" Be aware of those limiting thoughts that jump right to the top to happily let you know you can't do it! Who put these thoughts in your mind? Someone probably did it decades ago with their limiting point of view. But you have since grown up and became an independent person. Isn't it time for you to think your own thoughts?

How do we filter out unproductive, harmful thoughts? First, be aware of your thoughts. Then settle down and gently add other positive thoughts. Persistence is important. Baby steps will change your thoughts. Change your attitude and create a new reality for yourself.

October 30th

You got up this morning like other mornings. Almost unconsciously you went through your daily preparations and tasks. The power of habit is immense, but what about the limiting thoughts that go with it? Well, they repeat themselves too. So stop them! It's a new morning of a new day. There are new opportunities where we have the power to choose to let the drama go and focus on our thoughts and actions that will help us grow.

You have been given the opportunity to consciously choose what your day will look like. Choose wisely and consciously. Empower yourself and choose abundance, goodness, hope and responsibility for your life. It's less difficult than it seems; just change your mind in the morning and be aware of your thoughts. Take only what will make you blossom.

October 31th

Learn how to act for yourself.

Sometimes we find ourselves serving others in ways that make us give up on our principles and values, but it's not the right thing to do because ignoring our needs for others will make us resentful. Acting for ourselves can be a radical change from the way we've behaved so far. It is a matter of challenging the norms and doing what is best for us. If we continue to restrain ourselves and give up on our principals and desires then we will eventually feel like who we are is fading away.

It's instinct to act for yourself. You only have one life so why not live it for yourself? Of course, we have to have balance, so live life for yourself without the intention of becoming a narcissist. Like anything else in life, strive for balance.

November

November 1st

So, what is the basic truth of life?

Why are we here? What is our purpose? Is it to serve humanity, be innovators, and create breakthroughs to improve life? Or is our role to serve others and make them happy? All of these and more are external means of expression of the things that ultimately make us happy. Our purpose here, first and foremost, is to be happy. Happiness is an ongoing process. What matters are the small things that make you happy. Choose non-material things like spending time with your partner, walking on the beach, watching a movie, walking, playing basketball, swimming, drawing, singing, or dancing. Everyone has their list, be sure to pay attention to what truly makes *you* happy.

As an exercise, create a "happiness list" and write everything that you can think of that makes you happy. Next, set a goal for yourself to complete at least one activity per day. Make *this* a habit and then add more items to your list.

November 2nd

Life isn't a picnic, only a few people were born that lucky.

Most people that have become rich and famous got there by working hard and staying determined. They've definitely experienced many disappointments along the way, but carried on. Failures are part of the tuition to enter the School of Life. They tripped and fell, but got back up, shook the dust off and carried on. *This* is how you must think, feel and act.

Each and every one of us must have a goal for ourselves and understand the rules of the game we're playing to achieve it. The race is long and there's a lot of work, but it is always worth it. Work smart for that goal, it won't come without a struggle. We must be brave, strong and disciplined. We need to be determined that nothing can stand in the way of our goal.

True, we will meet those who will tell us that we'll fail, that we're not good or strong enough, that our ideas are silly and have already been done, or that we're too old. Anyways, why should things turn out well for you? *Remember!* It's **your** goal, **your** way and it's **yours**. Look directly at your goal and act decisively to achieve it. Find what drives you to make it happen.

What *is* your goal? Think about your biggest desires that are outside of your immediate reach. Think about what drives you or what will make you truly happy in the long run. Act tirelessly to achieve them. Start with small, measured steps and gradually take on bigger steps. Remember, Lao Tzu's, "A journey of a thousand miles begins with one small step".

November 3rd

Celebrate today. There's nothing special about it, but that's no reason to not celebrate! After a night's sleep, in which dreams process information and give us clues from the depth of our soul, the day is a new beginning. Decide today that you're free from the feelings of frustration, doubt, and stress from the behavior of yourself or others. Choose to walk with compassion and patience. Remember that everything is always okay. This is life, and it's okay even when we think it isn't. Treat yourself nicely. Remind yourself that you love yourself. You are okay the way you are, there's nothing to fix and no one to blame. You're doing what you can.

Celebrate your life today, you deserve it and it's yours.

November 4th

Choose who you want to be.

Sometimes it seems like life doesn't have a clear plan. People and life events can present hidden opportunities, but sometimes also difficulties. At any given moment we have the right to choose who we want to be: a victim or someone who is assertive and responsible for their own actions. The difference between these two choices is what will determine the quality of our lives. An assertive and responsible person understands that they have the right to choose and that they are responsible for their feelings at any given moment.

The choice sometimes comes at a price that requires dealing with the consequences alone, however it's a deliberately chosen path and how great is that! Then there's the victim, limited by their perceived choices, chained to their habits, blinded by their perceptions without having the ability to change them. The victim deprives themselves of freedom, but the profit gained is huge since they don't ever have to take responsibility. Someone else pays for everything, whether it's a partner, an employer, a family member, the government or God! But the person who is responsible, the victim, will never claim their responsibility and that's their decision. The person who bears their own responsibility will be much happier than the victim because they freely choose their own reaction to life's events.

So today, choose to be responsible for your destiny; it's a gift.

November 5th

Smile at the world and it will smile back.

I'm pretty sure that you've heard this saying more than once, but there's a lot of wisdom in those words. A human being is the only creature that has the ability to smile. There are reasons for it. A smile is inviting, it removes barriers and signals that there is no danger. The energy of a smile radiates outward. It can't be ignored and a radiant smile invites the good. You come equipped with a gift, use it more than you need to. This is one of the better gifts given to us.

Smile at the world and it will smile back. True, we don't always feel that we can or that we really want to smile, especially when circumstances are not in our favor, but a natural smile creates reconciliation with difficult times. A smile says, "Yes, the situation might be difficult, but there's hope and light at the end of the tunnel." Look at yourself in the mirror and realize how a smile can expand your heart and immediately make you happy. The symptoms should be closeness and affection. Use this resource more. Smile, smile, and see how the universe will smile back at you.

Do it now. Smile. It's fun and liberating. Be aware of how much better your soul feels.

All of this can happen even before you've encountered another person!

November 6th

If you are comfortable where you are then you are not growing, because growth only happens through effort.

This may contradict the advice I've offered in this book so far, but I want to share how to create harmony with ourselves and our surroundings, and how to best create the peace and calmness we are missing in our lives. I don't intend to sabotage your serenity, but new ideas are making their way into the world, realizations are born and our deepest desires make their way to the surface.

Life presents challenges. Even the beginning is difficult. See how arduous birth can be for both the mother and child. The baby fights its way through the narrow birth canal with all its tiny strength until it bursts into the world. Just like birth, growth in life must have a component of resistance or else we can't grow. Effort is a part of life and is a blessed thing. It makes us grow and gain experience that is essential for us to have.

There is an absolute truth that surrounds us, the most experienced sailors didn't gain their knowledge sailing in calm waters. Olympic athletics didn't go from their couches to the gold medal. Revolutionary ideas have to work their way through the fear to be heard. You must believe that making an effort is a natural act, not a bad thing. Put forward your *best* effort and allow yourself to fail, gain experience and try again.

We must understand that challenges are part of life and dealing with them is what makes life meaningful.

Think of something you want to achieve today, it doesn't have to be big. Asking for a vacation at work or asking someone you like to go on a date is enough. It's even enough to do an unpleasant task you've postponed for a while with all the excuses in the world- today's your day!

November 7th

A journey of a thousand miles begins with a single step.

Throughout this book I've emphasized how personal growth begins with a collection of small daily steps. I'm not a fan of large changes as I believe that as creatures of nature we are governed by ancient laws aimed at helping us survive. The strong survival mechanism inherent in us is called the fight or flight response. It helped us evolve when in a split second, the core adrenaline gland produced a hormonal waterfall that filled us up instantly, preparing us for lurking danger. For a moment we become Superman and we can protect ourselves or run away in a fraction of the time it normally takes. The wild animals and natural dangers were eventually replaced by cars and modernity. Today the fight or flight mechanism is activated in many cases that no longer involve life or death situations. Anxiety and stress have replaced those challenges.

One of the unbearable modern fears is speaking in front of an audience. Jerry Seinfeld said that research finds people are more scared of an audience than death, that's why at a funeral they'd rather be in the coffin than giving the eulogy. Apart from this crippling fear, people have other fears that activate their survival mechanism. It could be a conversation with their boss, talking to a person they have a crush on, or standing up for themselves. In all of these cases the survival mechanism is activated and causes goosebumps, sweating, a quickened heart rate and paralysis. In these cases, fright was the chosen response.

Daily readings of this book will allow you to improve and grow, and skip the flight or fight response. Determination and consistency are what creates positive change, and over time we'll realize how far we've come.

Choose one of the previous three days lessons and redo it.

November 8th

You woke up this morning! Say thank you.

Our problems begin when we take things for granted. That's a huge mistake, our lives are a miracle. Believe it or not you were born a champion. In the race to the egg you competed against millions of others and finished first! What is that if not a miracle?

You woke up this morning to a new day, everything else is a bonus. Be grateful for the miracle of life. Don't take it for granted, you've been lucky. Remember this and internalize the fact that you were born a champion. Look at the world from a different perspective.

Understand that there's no room for feelings of inferiority since you were born a winner. You proved your worth just by being born. You competed and won. Millions of others tried to fertilize the same egg and you finished first! You got the trophy – you've won a life!

November 9th

The main thing is to not be afraid.

Fear is sometimes a good servant, but often a bad master. Fear helps us cross the street safely and avoid things that can physically hurt us. Thus, fear serves us faithfully. When fear is our master it can bring damage and destruction. When fear controls us in situations that aren't life threatening it causes an excruciating feeling when we think about each missed opportunity. Our biggest fear should simply be forgetting to live.

In the Israeli Defense Force there is the concept of "striving for contact" which is contrary to our natural instinct to flee. Soldiers learn to ignore their fear and get up to attack their enemy. This may indeed be an extreme situation, but it does challenge fear.

For most of us, there aren't many life-threatening situations. In our daily lives scary situations can be as simple as talking about a raise, leaving a workplace, leaving a toxic relationship, asking someone you like on a date, etc. In fact, fear in these situations hurts us if we don't push through it. Those who take the risk and dare succeed, because these events are ultimately a natural part of our daily routine that we must learn to master.

Walk around with this insight: strive for contact and choose to be brave! Get over your fear and do one small "scary" thing each day. The results aren't relevant in the here and now, but the very act of taking the initiative is a win. True, sometimes your results aren't what you wanted, however, if you don't try there will be no opportunity for growth.

Pat yourself on the back for doing one thing today that scared you.

"The whole world is a very narrow bridge and the main thing is to not be afraid at all!"

Rabbi Nachman of Breslov.

November 10th

We run nowhere like mice on a wheel. There is a wheel reserved for each of us. Life can move quickly like a film, becoming a wearing and exhausting routine. Life's chores fill our time and does not allow us to stop and look around us or at us. It's time to stop the race and think.

A good friend of mine once told me that one Saturday he was sitting watching TV and suddenly someone blocked his vision. He looked at them and saw that they were going to his fridge, getting something to eat. Later he heard another noise and saw someone holding his phone talking. He asked himself, "Who are these people and what are they doing in my house?" This observation hit him like lightning on a clear day. Where was he all these years and how did he pay so little attention to his family? Exhausted and unhappy he decided to slow the pace and be present in his own life. It's so easy to be distracted today by cell phones, emails, and other technologies. The ease of availability has turned us all into slaves and the time passes faster when we disengage. Let's stop for a moment and take a look at ourselves and our surroundings so that we don't miss the gift of life, so that we don't wake up too late and ask ourselves, "Who are all these people around me?" Wake up now!

Today, be present. Breathe deeply and say "I am here" and pay attention to what is happening around you. Slow your pace down and live in the moment without past or future getting in the way. Be present here and now. Be present, slowly.

November 11th

If I had to summarize all the books on self-fulfillment and motivation in one sentence I would undoubtedly cite Greg S. Reid, "A dream written down with a date becomes a goal. A goal broken down into steps becomes a plan. A plan backed by action makes your dreams come true."

In the end, everything is simple, but sometimes because it is so simple that we can't see it. We think that all solutions should be complex and that something needs to be studied for a long time to be understood. Each of us has dreams, but are they all achievable? Any dream (within human limitations) can be fulfilled. Every realistic dream you've dreamed of someone somewhere has fulfilled it. Unusual dreams can come true, but to make them come true requires extraordinary vision. Are you ready for the high prices you will have to pay?

Turning a dream into a series of small and measured steps will get you there. Always act with perseverance, determination and patience.

Will you attempt to make your dreams come true? At most you will succeed!

November 12th

Do you have a problem that you are trying to solve?

It's really bothering you and you need the solution now. Demanding a solution may work for you, but it won't always work the way you expect it to. How about just letting go and having your great brain find the solution? In the quiet and stillness of deep thought your mind will find an answer, but it will be on its own terms. Your mind needs time and you need to stop resisting. Relax, let go and dream. There's an obedient part within you that's waiting for ideal conditions so that it can serve you the solutions you were looking for on a silver platter. The brain asks for just one thing: patience. Give it time and it will find the solution.

So when you have a problem, trying to find a solution forcefully may have the opposite effect you want. You, as a *whole* system, are stressed. Stress hormones activate your fight or flight response which dulls the thoughts and creativity needed to find solutions.

Wait, stay calm and be patient. Close your eyes and rest your mind. Let the answers find you.

November 13ᵗʰ

Do your actions propel you forward?

This is a question I have learned to consciously ask myself. The distractions around us are endless. At any moment something flashes across the screen that catches our attention. Another email has been received, another text message was sent. It's easy to forget about our path and indulge in these distractions. But does it advance us? This is a question I consistently and consciously ask myself, and the answer is always clear. Sometimes I don't want to hear it, but I know that in order to reach my goals I need to answer with an honest and courageous heart. I ask myself this question not only when I'm distracted, but also when I'm in an argument. After all, it's very easy to let the ego take over and destroy and devastate. But does it help me? Not really. I ask myself that question and then come up with some conscious choices: I can either choose to continue on the same path that feeds my monster ego or find another way that will move me forward in a healthy way.

Consciously ask yourself this question. You will be happy with the results!

November 14th

Just live.

Sometimes we are so preoccupied with all the details in our lives that we forget to live. What is life if it isn't here and now? Worries and regrets exist in the past and have no place in the present. The easiest way to get rid of these emotions is to ignore them and live in the present moment.

Sometimes the people around us can seem so different, but apart from their memories and experiences, we're all the same. We're all having one common experience. Life is waiting for us silently and patiently hoping that we'll truly engage and thrive. Worries, fears and regret have no place in the present. Take a deep breath, go with the flow and accept your reality. If you're thinking and learning then everything will be alright. Now go and have a lovely day :-)

November 15th

What are you focusing on?

Do you focus on your failures and mistakes? Are you filled with a sense of missing out or feeling small, helpless and like giving up? It's easy to focus on those things. In fact, most people are focused on their shortcomings. They're engaged in self-flagellation and addicted to misery. This unhappiness can draw sympathy from our friends and family and the reward can be immense: understanding and attention. But the reward is only short term and ultimately our feelings don't improve in the long run.

We should be focused on our success. Relive those moments of triumphs instead of the moments of failure. Learn to live in your successes instead of failures. Learn to think positively. What did you do well yesterday and what are you doing well today? You always have something that you are doing well in. Even though friends and family are a huge wave of support in the short term, success comes with inner satisfaction and the knowledge that you can rely on yourself.

If you focus on your success you'll eventually see that you don't need understanding and attention from others. You'll learn to trust yourself, and what a wonderful feeling that is!

November 16th

Success.

Endless words have been written (and are still being written) about it. So how do you achieve success and how do you maintain it? Success has three main components: perseverance, commitment and proactivity. This is the entire concept in short. It isn't simple, but is failure simpler?

Successful people think this way whether they are aware of it or not. If you want to be successful in anything you must practice those rules until it becomes second nature. Perseverance is a crucial part. As the famous saying goes, "90% of success is just showing up." Commitment is the other motivator to be proactivity. Maintaining success is done through daily learning and continuous improvements in your chosen field.

It's not hard. It's actually easier than staying stuck. It makes you want to be better for yourself.

Do it!

November 17th

Leave the drama to movies and TV shows.

Some of us are addicted to drama. It allows us to feel alive and included. It's even a way to control others. What's behind the need for drama? Is it loneliness or fear? Why not leave the drama and the people who create it behind? Surround yourself with positive people, people who are full of joy for life and who laugh and have fun. Drama is usually accompanied by accusations and focusing on evil. A life without drama is a loving and happier life.

Do you understand what you're losing when you create and are part of the drama? It's just another bad movie! How will your life look from today onwards? I've chosen, what about you?

November 18th

Start with a banana.

Every change comes with resistance. The desire to change is sometimes paralyzing. It's not for nothing that the journey of a thousand miles begins with one small step. The ancient sages recognized that the most difficult part of change is the first step. Therefore, the easiest way to make a big change is through small changes. I followed this way of thinking when I changed my diet. I took small steps until it became a habit.

I start the day with a banana or another piece of fruit. I don't think about it, I just do it. It's become second nature and guess what? Now I eat an additional 365 fruits per year.

What is your "banana"? What little change will you make every day that will become 365 changes per year?

November 19th

You may be holding a copy of this book or reading it on your phone, tablet or computer.

If you're traveling by public transportation stop for a moment and take a look at all those who take advantage of this spare time. Put down the distractions for a moment and just be present. Take a deep breath, exhale slowly and just watch. This is a much more effective use of your time.

November 20th

It doesn't matter what came before, where you came from, where you were born, the color of your skin or which gender you identify with!

What matters is what you think about it! The good news is that every morning you can reinvent yourself and create a new reality. It isn't easy or simple, but probably better than giving up and unconsciously walking a path that leads nowhere.

You can take responsibility for your life, you can navigate it and you can choose your path. Yes, you!

November 21th

I have learned that one of the forces that changes reality is the power of perseverance.

Sometimes we dream of something, take action to try and get it and then, after only a short time, lose the energy and desire to continue. It's similar to the way a match is lit, the flame at first is intense and then it is slowly weakened by the wind until it's extinguished. Where does success end and failure begin? Rabbi Akiva wondered about the formation of wells and realized that, "A water droplet cuts through rock not by virtue of its *power*, but by virtue of its *perseverance.*" Life is made up of different sections, some of which we'll rejoice in and be happy about, and others where we'll experience despair.

The power of perseverance lets us overcome obstacles in this journey called life.

November 22th

90% of success is just showing up.

We wanted to show, but we didn't. We couldn't make that bold move. What is a bold move? It's a move that involves risk. And what is the risk? It's beating down the ego that will do anything to protect itself, even at the cost of halting your growth. Remember that in the end the bold wins. Win to beat the doubt in you, the paralyzing fear and threatening anxiety. Success through bold and courageous steps will lift you up a notch. In hindsight you won't even remember what was so scary. Don't let your fears stop you from showing up. Go and everything else will work itself out.

If you leap into the water and swim then you've already done 90% of the work to succeed.

November 23th

When you give up, who are you giving up for?

Is it for your boss or your spouse, or just giving up on life? There's nothing wrong with giving up when it's done consciously and out of empathy and compassion. Giving up is meant to protect you and leave you in your familiar comfort zone. It's okay to give up, but not when it's out of fear, anxiety or the need to please. This type of giving up is like compound interest; it accumulates frustration, helplessness, feelings of inferiority, etc. If this is the kind of giving up you do then know that you are giving up on yourself. Why should you do that when others would be happy to watch you give up?

Remember that wherever you go you'll probably step on someone's toes, just be careful not to step on your own. Stop giving up on yourself and live life because you deserve it, and that's the truth.

November 24th

Where are you now?

Look around you. Life doesn't seem as simple as it used to be, but in fact, it's simpler. The life of a cave dweller simpler, but they still had to hunt for their next meal. Now, you can walk into a grocery store or restaurant and get a gourmet meal. And for a drink, in the worst case, you can turn on your faucet and get tap water, and in the best case you can open a bottle of mineral water. What are your circumstances? Einstein said that everything is relative, so compare your life to that of the cave dweller. You'll be pleasantly surprised. You'll actually be so surprised that you'll be grateful. For some examples: https://howrichami.givingwhatwecan.org/how-rich-am-i

Do yourself a favor and say thank you!

November 25th

Do you want to succeed?
You can't get there by sitting down or staying in your comfort zone. We grow and develop by entering new territory where we aren't comfortable. We need to leave the familiar and ordinary. We can look at challenges as either something to fear and a reason to run back to our comfort zone or we can look at it with courage as an opportunity. Ultimately, results are in the discomfort zone. Your reward is breaking the imaginary boundaries you have made for yourself.

Growth, pride, satisfaction and feelings of invincibility await. Get up now and do it. At maximum you will succeed.

November 26th

Where is the divine spirit? Do we need intermediaries? Has someone received the power of attorney to represent God on earth?

Every one of us has a divine spark waiting to be revealed. We're made up of stardust, we all come from the same cosmic substance. In the book of Exodus 25:8 it says, "And let them make me a sanctuary; that I may dwell among them." In my opinion this verse is confirmation that the Divine lives within us. Remember that Satan shouts and God whispers. Call it intuition, but there's something in us that helps us. We shouldn't fear it, we need to believe in it. The more you ask for something, the more these forces will give. Think of what goes on behind those great cosmic forces. Are your requests something that the powers cannot grant you? Thinking of yourself as unimportant is irrational or thinking that you don't matter to the flow of Universal energy is absurd.

The Divine is within you, find it and then use it.

November 27th

I was sitting at an airport terminal waiting for a flight that would take me to a conference when Celine Dion's songs played through my headphones. A person with a disability sits in the chair next to me. They have a walker. All of a sudden, I am struck by gratitude that I'm healthy and can walk without assistance. I thank him in my heart for allowing me to cherish my health. I thank my good fortune that I am healthy and I'm full of gratitude. If you get up every morning healthy everything else is just a bonus.

It reminds me of a video I once saw about a driver who was sitting at a traffic light looking at the Ferrari next to him. He expressed that he wished he had a car like that. At the next intersection there was a motorcycle next to him, who looked at his car wishing that one day he too would have one. At the next intersection a cyclist is next to the motorcycle and they wished for a motorcycle. A man runs past them and looks at the bicycle and wishes for such a bike. From one of the buildings that overlooks the intersection a disabled person in a wheelchair overlooks them all and wishes that he could put on sneakers and run.

Take nothing for granted!

November 28th

In the Western world (and perhaps in the entire world) the answer to happiness has been consumerism.

Commercials compete with each other and try in every way to motivate us to buy their brand that guarantees us momentary happiness. This happens when we open a new package. We feel supreme happiness, it feels so good! But after a while the effect wears off and we find ourselves again in a shopping frenzy to get that momentary happiness back. It's a failed method to happiness because we lose that feeling so quickly. We are in an addictive endless buying frenzy that impoverishes us and increases our debts.

When Alexander the Great looked at all the territories he had conquered his heart was filled with sadness because there were no more territories left to capture. Happiness lies in doing valuable acts out of righteousness. Help others, open your heart and fill it with unconditional love. Be thankful for the lessons you've learned, humbly observe life and cherish your experiences. Happiness is knowing that we are loved and cherished. Objects won't make us happier, but our values, impact and the inspiration we can give others will make us content!

Be a source of inspiration, find your meaning and love those around you. Remember to open your heart.

November 29th

Rebirth brings us new opportunities, and it's something that happens every morning when you wake up. Why not take initiative and become the creator of your day? Either way, even if we don't take the initiative, we are the ones who create our day, most of us without any conscious thought. Usually, the result is less than desirable when it's not intentional.

Create your day intentionally. It will be wonderful because you made it yourself.

November 30th

The universe is everything.

You're a part of it and it doesn't judge you. In fact, it doesn't matter if you're the President of the United States or a rebellious poor person in India, to the Universe we're all the same. The Universe's resources are here for you. We're all human beings and the differences between us are unimportant. Our genetic codes are similar and we all operate the same. The biggest differences are our circumstances. But should those differences dictate our success or failure?

It's true that some of us have more comfortable, war-free and carefree lives that makes following the right path easier. Circumstances cannot be controlled, but our approach to them determines whether we will transcend our challenges or be defeated. Whoever succeeds will grow and whoever secedes will fade. What are you going to choose?

December

December 1st

Avoidance.

It's so tempting to avoid. It's far easier to stay in our comfort zones. Conflict is never comfortable. Sometimes, we just prefer to ignore our problems. We try to get around our issues without resolving them. Have you ever tried to avoid talking to your partner about a problematic issue? For a while it may seem that things are okay, but your avoidance will most likely lead to confrontation anyway. Avoiding a problem doesn't make it disappear, it just stalls time and allows the problem to grow to monstrous proportions by feeding on our procrastination.

We are not alone. Compromises and decisions will be made, but do yourself a favor and change the habit of avoidance. Today, strive for contact. You'll profit since the initiative came from you. Keep your conflicts small. *Now* you are taking responsibility for your life.

December 2nd

Sometimes there's friction between who we are and who we'd like to be.

This tension can come out in extreme or stressful situations, or when we're frustrated by something that we've said or done. Of course, we'll want to go back in time and change our mistakes, however, we cannot. So, in those situations it's best to let the frustration dissipate and allow compassion and forgiveness to permeate us. We're only human. We aren't perfect and we will make mistakes. We'll be dishonest and crazy. Chances are we will continue to disappoint someone!

This is part of the human condition. If we accept and understand that then it will save us future heartbreak, frustration and disappointment. We can use our imagination to see us as our best selves, as the person we want to be. The more we try to behave like that person the more likely it is that we will become that person. Our willpower and imagination can turn us into the person we've been dreaming of becoming.

Think about difficult situations you may encounter and plan your reactions and behavior to the event. Even though this exercise may be hard at first, continue on as this will help you act as your best self.

December 3rd

What's good about pressure? What is it useful for?

Is it our blood pressure, our heart that's working hard or our skin? Modern life dictates that we have loaded schedules acting like acrobats in a circus that have to do several things at once, (especially when the family is involved). In this rat race there are no winners! The material rewards could leave spiritual voids, family destruction, depression or addiction to medication. Is it worth it? You do the math. Our happiness doesn't depend on this rat race. On the contrary, reducing stress and doing things at your own pace makes you happier.

You might think that this race is a necessity, but if you look closely you'll see that you've probably brought this on yourself. The expenses and obligations aren't all necessary. They lie in wanting to consume far beyond the existing capacity. Slow down, be aware, breathe deeply, and reduce the background noise. The immediate payoff is that your life will stop moving so quickly. A nervous breakdown or a heart attack is surely the result of a stressful lifestyle. Balance is achieved when you stop, observe and be present. When you slow down you feel the present moment and this moment increases joy, vitality and calm wisdom.

Today, slow down, look around, smell, observe, breathe deeply and be aware of your presence here and now. Practice this and see how much more clarity you have.

December 4th

Choose wisely.

You've probably heard this many times. Choosing wisely is having the option to drive distracted, but choosing to drive focused. At any given moment we have a range of possibilities. An argument with a specific person can develop into rage with yelling, a thunderous silence, or God forbid, violence. On the other hand, choosing wisely with the understanding that there are other opinions, will allow you to create a bridge for communication with the other person, accepting what they're offering and in a cultivated manner, navigating towards the desired results. There are so many different ways to react in every situation. Our ego always wants to win, or even wants to destroy the opponent and damage their ego. Our wisest path here is to practice choosing the best response. And what is that? This is where wisdom comes in, helping us choose the response that will let us achieve what we want. If we've achieved the opposite result then we probably chose on the side of stupidity.

Today, practice choosing wisely because only good will come of it, and the ego, ours and theirs, will recover.

December 5th

Do things with awareness.
Who brushed your teeth this morning? Who tied your shoe-laces? When it comes to our daily routines we often go on autopilot. It saves us time and brain power and lets us turn our awareness to other things. It's a wonderful mechanism whose entire function is to help with daily routines. It's comfortable, easy and effortless so it's easy to be tempted into allowing it to do more than needed.

Moderation is the key to everything, in this case as well. Life is happening here and now, in this moment. Being on autopilot makes these moments unimportant and prevents us from being present. Awareness is the key to preventing this. Awareness is the complete opposite of the automatic. Having awareness of thoughts, feelings and actions allows us to experience life intensely.

Allow autopilot to take over when performing daily tasks that you have no investment in. Let it tie your shoes and lock the door, but when something matters to your soul, wake up and be present. Let your awareness be your guide!

December 6th

Recently...

The film industry has been filled with superheroes. Starting with the revival of Superman, continuing with X-Men, Supergirl, Batman, Guardians of the Galaxy, Wonder Woman, etc. Their popularity comes at a time when there is a lack of responsible adults controlling the chaos around the world. How easy would it be if there was someone powerful and without limitations, to fix all the destruction left behind? Sometimes we childishly crave superpowers and superheroes to protect us when we feel hurt, weak or used.

We all have superhero characteristics, it's a fact. Prominent traits superheroes have are invulnerability and a quick ability to recover. If we could only adopt those qualities we'd be superheroes ourselves. But we can only become our own heroes once we've accepted ourselves, with our advantages and disadvantages, as simply human. Understand that we must be compassionate with ourselves. We must learn to live in peace with and love ourselves for who we are- humans, miracles of creation. Once we hold these beliefs then it will be almost impossible to hurt us, undermine our confidence or manipulate us. It's not easy to get there, but daily practice of positive thinking, deep breathing, and meditation will bring us much closer.

Love yourself. Forgive yourself and others. Discover the superpowers laying dormant within you. Start now!

December 7th

Who do you want to be?

We all have a vision of ourselves, usually one that is much more positive than how we really are. There's only one problem with this illusion and that's the future will one day become our present. This elusiveness mocks us with the hope that one day we'll be able to fulfill this vision. In the meantime, life keeps at its regular pace.

Stop for a moment and look around, be present in the moment and think about who you want to be. Regardless of the passing time or the future we must take responsibility and direct ourselves step by step towards the person we want to become. If we don't change our course of negativity, life is guaranteed to mold us into a different person than the one we want to be. The process begins with awareness, the mental picture has to be clear. If you follow these directions your thoughts will slowly manifest and become your present.

Today, stop for a few minutes. Sit with yourself and think about who you'd like to be. Imagine that you are already there.

December 8th

Learn to cherish.

The intensity and often the abrasiveness of our routine blinds us from the potential goodness in our life. In these situations it's very easy to grumble, blame the world, the weather, the politicians, everyone else and even ourselves. I'm sure that throughout your life you've complained to yourself, "I'm lazy, I'm fat, I'm stupid, I'm a loser."

But what about all the things you've achieved? Don't compare yourself to other people because there will always be someone who has more than you.

Today, make a mental list of things you have achieved. I'm sure you'll find it to be longer than you thought. Think of what you've achieved in terms of health, family, friends, career, education, love and support.

Challenge yourself to think of the small things you've done and never acknowledged. Let the list grow. As time passes it will only get bigger.

Mentally continue to update the list and let it grow. Think about it when your accomplishments aren't obvious to you! Compliment yourself. You deserve it.

December 9th

Starting Over!

We are all given the opportunity to start over. This isn't about a long-term offer or another opportunity that has come our way. In fact, we start fresh every day when we wake up in the morning.

That isn't a cliche.

The transition from yesterday to today is as important to the soul as it is important to the body. During sleep we go through cleansing, resetting and information processing. The nightly break of a few hours allows the body and soul to relax and get ready for the new day. When we get up in the morning, all opportunities and choices are open to us. Remember that regardless of any temporary difficulties, what makes the difference is how we approach it. Circumstances exist in their own right and often, regardless of our participation, control is usually out of the question. All we have left to do is to start over, remembering the miracle of life. Your presence here is in the image of God.

See today as another opportunity given to you. This opportunity repeats itself every day. Be aware that the choice of how to live your life is yours. So, start over and see this day as an opportunity.

December 10th

Get off the chair. Sometimes that's all it takes, yet it can be so difficult or even impossible.

Many of the limitations in our lives stem from our perception of reality. However, there is no relationship between our perception of reality and actual reality. We limit ourselves because of how we feel and think.

There is a well-known story about a circus elephant tied to a thin wooden pole. The elephant doesn't try to break free even though it could with little effort. When the elephant was a baby it tried to pull the pole out of the ground, but all its efforts were in vain. Even though over the years the elephant grew and became stronger its perceptions about the pole stayed the same. The memory of helplessness continued to hold weight over the elephant and it no longer tried to break free from the pole. The elephant convinced itself that it wouldn't be able to. However, this way of thinking has nothing to do with the current reality. It's the elephant's mistaken belief that dictates its behavior, the belief that it couldn't break free so there was no point in trying. It's a trap that we all fall into and it pervades our lives. Bitter past experiences prevent us from trying because failure has been burned into our hearts and minds. We have the responsibility to challenge these misguided perceptions and thoughts. All we need is to get off the chair and see that the reason we didn't get up in the first place was due to our thoughts, not reality.

Choose one action today that you're not sure you can do and try to do it!

Maybe you'll succeed this time!

December 11ᵗʰ

Let's touch on happiness.

What hasn't been written about happiness? It's elusive, it's dependent on something else, it's an illusion and it's disappointing. It's an ideal concept, a kind of Utopia that only exists in a parallel universe between reality and a concept that is like a deep abyss. Many search for happiness. Some "find" it through material items. It could be a collection of impressive shoes. Each shoe bought causes the level of happiness to soar, but after a while it dives back down. Endless shopping can cause a glimpse of happiness, but that happiness is short lived. Between each purchase is where the hidden abyss lies. Addiction has a tendency to create short bursts of happiness even if that isn't what we really long for. Happiness like that isn't a result of our efforts.

How do we keep ourselves from doing that? First learn to rely on yourself and forgive yourself. Understand that everything is okay even when it isn't. There will be easy periods and there will be difficult periods. Sometimes the skies will be gloomy, but eventually the sun will penetrate the clouds and warm up your heart.

Second, understand that you are thinking at every single moment, even if you aren't aware of it. Learn to watch your thoughts and slowly direct your thoughts towards growth, compassion, love, forgiveness, understanding and inclusion. Happiness doesn't depend on external factors but on your ability to control your thoughts and think optimistically.

Today pay attention to your thoughts, listen to the inner dialog happening tirelessly in your mind. Gently command and direct your thoughts towards growth, understanding and acceptance. Watch as the level of your happiness slowly grows.

December 12th

How do you spend your time?

I remember reading a study about how our lives are divided. The data wasn't appealing. A third of our lives are spent sleeping- I don't see that as a waste of time though because that's when our body and brain are resting and processing information. A chronic lack of sleep causes problems such as pre-depressive states, nervousness, lack of concentration, restlessness and impairment of the metabolism. A waste of time is being in traffic jams, lines and staring at brainwashing commercials. Our attention is stolen by a small and "smart" device that sweeps us away through our fingertips. You must understand how much you would grow if you invested some of that stolen time into your personal growth.

Instead of staring at a screen for a few hours a day, take a small portion of that time and meditate for a few minutes, read a book, or practice your breathing. It will make a difference. It's not something you need to invest a lot of time in, prioritize quality time over destroying precious brain cells.

Do it today! Replace your stolen time with something that will lead you to growth.

December 13th

So, who are we?

We're probably a result of our behavior pattern. What is their origin? Our past. Some psychologists claim that they originated in childhood and others even claim that our personality was shaped in the womb. If so, what can we do about it? Well, we have the potential to change. And what can we change? Who we can be. We can live without fear and doubts and instead with courage and faith in ourselves. Where is the potential? It is in the future. We can adopt patterns of behavior from the future.

The future contains your potential, which is everything you can be. The best version of you exists in the future, but you can bring it to the present.

December 14th

Today, practice improving your life by only planting positive thoughts. Remember that at any given moment there is only one thought in your mind. Why not make it a positive thought. Thoughts create your reality. So, let's practice making our realities amazing!

Warning!! Side effects can be severe and may include vitality, joy and self-love. You've been warned!

December 15th

Today we'll focus on fear.

What hasn't been said about it? Many books have been written about it. Many psychologists owe their livelihood to it. University faculties are full of students and professors trying to figure out how it works. But here on this page I will tell you my theory.

Without fear our lives would be changed beyond recognition. Most likely, we would have injured ourselves by now and destroyed our surroundings because without fear we have no warning system. Without fear, what would prevent us from jumping off a tall building or taking whatever we want from a store? Beyond being "culturally adapted" we have an internal fear of the consequences of our actions.

So, fear has great value, but it also prevents us from gaining self-fulfillment. Fear is valuable if we use the correct dosage. What's the point of living life afraid of what other people think? What's the point of living a life that everyone else enjoys except us? We have the responsibility to explore our boundaries and break through barriers of fear that suppress us physically and mentally. Shakespeare once said "A coward dies a thousand times before his death, but the valiant taste of death but once." We die only once, but the coward dies hundreds of times. Is there any worth in these futile deaths? Not anything I can see.

We must dare to face our fears and here is where the true nature of courage comes in. Courage doesn't mean *acting* without fear, but in *spite* of fear. Boundaries drawn in our lives are determined by our courage. We must act with courage because, in the end, most people regret the things they didn't do, not the things they did.

Today decide to do something brave. I promise you that the attempt will make you stronger.

December 16ᵗʰ

Happiness cannot be saved or stored. Like drug addicts we wake each morning and go to sleep each night hoping for a little more happiness.

Today: Stop for a moment and think, what do I *really* need? Will my next purchase be the one that will improve my quality of life forever and make me happier? Is the next purchase necessary or is it intended to satisfy yet another need that can't be satisfied? Stop, think, decide. Is it worth it?

December 17ᵗʰ

Are you trying to impress?

Since childhood we have tried to impress others and relish in the acknowledgement of our achievements. We all want our parents to be proud of us when we're kids. This desire follows us throughout our lives. For some of us, seeking approval becomes a career. Some buy luxury apartments and some buy shiny new cars. It's okay if you can afford it, but in every purchase like that there's a higher price to pay. Sometimes the price is financial and sometimes it's compromising on our identity. Did we marry someone because that's what our parents wanted? Is the career we've chosen the one of our dreams or is it the one that pleases other people the most? Sometimes in our need to impress we've forgotten to impress the most important person in the world. Ourselves. *Is this what I really want?*

Ask yourself today, what do I and only I want? Check whether your decisions get you closer to your wants or if there is still a long way to go. Make choices that will shorten the distance. Remember that as far as we know, we live only once. Carpe Diem. Seize the day!

December 18th

We must remember that we're all ultimately stardust.

Our genetics are the same and the differences between us is only a fraction of one percent. So, in the end we're all pretty much the same. Our differences aren't so great. In practice this means that we aren't inferior to others. If we're jealous of others, if we feel inferior to others, it's not because of our differences, but it's because we have so little faith in ourselves.

We must strengthen our self-esteem and reduce the jealousy that exists within us. Jealousy is our inner demon that reveals our weakest spots and dark emotions that torment and shield us in a distorted way. We must focus on ourselves and think about how we can strive to be better, what we must do to grow and how to walk the same path as those we envy.

Remember, we're all pretty much the same. We're all stardust so there's almost no difference between us genetically. As individuals we're allowed to, and we owe it to ourselves, to do everything within our power to live fully!

December 19th

Do you understand what your opportunities are?

NASA telescopes have been monitoring the universe for decades and so far there is no trace of other life forms. What are the chances of discovering another life form? Earth is just far enough from the sun to allow life. It has a slope that allows seasons. It's partnered with our moon which allows for tides and earth's inclination. The moon also enables seasons. The earth's nucleus rotates and produces a magnetic field that protects living things from destructive solar radiation. Pay attention to how many variables must work together harmoniously to create an environment that supports life.

Earth is a lone inhabited planet, in one galaxy (one of many) within our solar system at the edge of the Milky Way. Out of all the infinite possibilities, we were created! Isn't that a miracle? So why take life for granted? Shouldn't we take the time to reflect on the miracle of our existence and understand its greatness and our own greatness? What are the chances? You've already won the lottery of life. Understand that and act accordingly.

December 20th

Life is full of unsolved mysteries and that's how it should be.
We won't ever be able to understand what infinity is, the meaning of time, or whether there was a beginning to everything. We don't have all the answers but it doesn't mean that we should suffer for it. In a personal sense, we sometimes find it difficult to understand those around us and even ourselves. Why do we choose to be frustrated when we could surrender and accept things as they are?

Today practice accepting your partner, those around you and yourself as you are. Feel the tension dissipate, tension that has built up because of our inability to understand. All that's left is to humbly accept our circumstances, other people and ourselves. You must accept reality lovingly because that's all there is, and that's enough.

December 21th

How are things going?

A wise man once said that if he divided people into two groups one would be full of intelligent people who have self-doubt and the other would be fools full of self-confidence. You probably know who ends up on top. I, of course, exaggerate the situation and am ignoring other factors, but this is to emphasize a certain feeling we sometimes experience.

December 22th

Children learn how to say "I don't want to."

Their choices are limited and their schedule is dictated by adults that are continuously making them unhappy. "Come eat." "I don't want to, I'm in the middle of a game." "Turn off the TV and do your homework" "I don't want to, this is my favorite show." It seems as if kids are overpowered with what adults expect of them, however, whether they are aware of it or not, eventually they are solely responsible for their lives.

The words "I don't want to" and "I can't" are embedded in our consciousness and often grow into more sophisticated phrases like, "It's impossible." "I don't have the right skills." "This is for someone younger/older/better than me." These phrases are obstacles that we create for ourselves. It's a refined way of saying, "I don't want to."

Out of habit and risk avoidance it's easier to say, "I don't want to" to many things. Wherever our thoughts are is where we'll ultimately end up.

Today: with childhood behind us, we must change our language from "I don't want to" to "what do I want?" Track and be aware of your thoughts. Make sure that the language is changing. You're a responsible adult when you ask yourself, "What do I really want?"

December 23th

Life is happening now, and now and... now.

It's happening every moment. Most people are waiting for better days and at the end of their lives they find it hard to remember everything that came before. They were always so busy waiting for something other than themselves to change. The moments between the beginning of our lives and the end are life itself.

It doesn't make sense to wait for the right partner to come along, or the right job, a better home, a great project, or retirement to start living. Waiting for the right moment to live your life is futile, it will never come. You have been alive since your first breath and you are wasting God's time if you are not living all that you can. It's a fact that our lives will end, but it's our choice on how to spend the time we're given.

Life is now. We do have a beginning and an end, but we only really have right now. Go through every moment breathing life into your lungs. Look around you, look up at the sky and smell the roses. That's what we have and that is life.

December 24th

All actions have a price that must be considered.

Not all profits are positive and sometimes the price we pay is unreasonable. Often, we are willing to denigrate our character just to punish and hurt the one we're fighting with. Our gain in this case is nothing more than the satisfaction knowing that we've caused pain to another person. The cost is that we've shown that we can be uncaring and unkind. The cost is the relationship, and how we feel about ourselves when all is said and done. The tension and anger are exhausting and in the long run causes lasting damage.

Think about the consequences before taking certain actions. Do those consequences contribute to your well-being? We need to practice minimizing the number of times we hurt ourselves or those around us just to satisfy our ego in the short term. It's easy to destroy ourselves and our world without realizing how hard it would be to rebuild.

Every time you come to a crossroad, breathe deeply and think about your well-being. What is the price and is it worth it?

December 25ᵗʰ

Is 24 hours not enough for you either?

The average number of hours of sleep has decreased significantly in recent decades. It's common to know someone who sleeps less than 6 hours a night. There's a lot to accomplish in one day and despite the high number of hours we spend awake and busy, the paradox is that life goes by much faster. Lack of sleep has negative effects on the body such as impairment of cognitive abilities, obesity, high blood pressure, insomnia, depression and other illnesses that are associated with lack of sleep.

Why don't we have enough time? Modern life gets in the way. Screens blur the hours between work and sleep. We sit and stare at pixels that take over our spare time. It's a symptom of a much more serious illness – "the avoidance of life". We have endless ways to distract ourselves and escape. Escape makes it possible to ignore the important questions and thoughts and ignore the responsibility we have for our life and happiness.

When we're too busy to think, we don't need to deal with the sad aimlessness of our lives or with the fear of our inevitable end. When we're busy we're on high alert and constantly sabotaging our happiness. The result is chronic fatigue, health problems, irritability and stress. Is it worth it? Paradoxically, in order to make time for ourselves we must slow down, sleep more and live in the present.

Slow down. Nothing external will change while you sleep. When rested you'll notice how life is rosy again. Accept the change.

December 26th

Out of my desire to develop and grow spiritually, I've refined many insights I've gathered over the years. Much of the information here is intuitive and has been made comprehensive. For every topic presented in this book you can find endless resources about it, but it's important to remember that the information you're not using isn't worth anything. Reading is enjoyable, but its effects are marginal if you don't apply it.

Daily practice will create spiritual growth and development. Bodybuilders don't reach their goals by reading about exercise. Determination and self-belief are what allows them to fulfill their vision. Just like them, you should follow a path. Take what's written and turn it into a daily habit using baby steps.

For example, when I worked on my nutrition to make it healthier I started with small dietary changes. I started to eat one piece of fruit every morning, and that equaled 365 more fruits per year that I wasn't eating before. If I added *any* servings of vegetables to a meal, I ate an additional few thousand vegetables per year. In the long run these small changes have had a dramatic impact on my health and none required a huge investment of energy or time. My changes were small, but they still required commitment to change a little every day. Change, even if little, can cause people to give up and go back to their old habits. But, without change we are left without benefit.

I invite you to read this book *every* day and apply the lessons in your life. Change will come slowly. Spiritual growth will become part of your being. In a year from now when you look back you will see the tremendous growth you've made in reaching your potential.

December 27th

Human operated software.

The basis of any program is coding. Coding, the language software programs use, is binary. It consists of only two digits: zero and one. From this one language, many other programming languages have emerged. Gradually, programming languages have become more sophisticated, but at its core it's still just zeroes and ones.

To understand our behavior we must become familiar with our make-up: thoughts, emotions, actions and results. Emotions originate from our thoughts and become the basis of our actions. Our actions then produce results. So, to change the results we're getting, all we have to do is change our thoughts. A change in thought patterns requires awareness. Awareness requires consistent daily practice.

Think about the power you have now! You have been given the key to the code that can change your life. With this code you can take an active part in changing your thoughts, emotions, actions and therefore the results that you achieve. Isn't that amazing?

Take responsibility for your thoughts by examining every one of them. It won't feel natural at first, but slowly you'll be able to master them. This will lead you to success.

December 28th

Our minds are constantly bombarded by our thoughts.

But there is only room for one thought at a time. Most thoughts are like glaciers; a tiny bit lives above the water and the majority of it lives below the sea. These are the thoughts that shape our personalities and behaviors. Thoughts create emotions, which dictates our actions and creates results. This is the process we've been perfecting in this book.

If we aren't satisfied with our results it is our responsibility to investigate how we arrived where we are. We must examine the actions that led us there and what emotions and thoughts motivated us to get there. Positive thoughts equal positive emotions. That will create positive results which inevitably causes happiness.

Practice this today. I'm sure the opportunity will arise.

December 29th

Sometimes we wake up and the sky is grey.
The clouds block the sunlight and everything feels less inspiring. But nothing has really changed, just your perspective. We're not always able to rationalize with ourselves and sometimes it's difficult to change our thoughts, but we have to keep in mind that the sky's still blue behind the clouds and tomorrow, when the sun is out, we'll see the results of today.

So, look up! The sun is always there, even if a few clouds are blocking it. Listen to your favorite music, read a good book and wait for a change to come.

December 30th

You've probably heard the phrase "No pain, no gain."

It may be obvious to you, but there are still many who hear this phrase, yawn, and turn their heads. They don't want to acknowledge it's worth. Be honest about the amount of effort you're putting in. Measure it and appreciate it. This is the best way to create a positive life and succeed. Growth occurs through consistent effort and breaking boundaries.

The most prominent example of this is obtaining financial wealth. Those who have built financial wealth through their own sweat and blood may put different values on their hard-earned worth than those who have inherited theirs. There are those who put a lot of effort into tending their wealth and increasing their portfolio values by tenfold. On the other hand, as many as one-third of all lottery winners will go bankrupt within five years due to overspending and poor money management. Do you think that the lottery winners would have increased and managed their wealth differently if they had earned their money through work instead of luck?

Take the time to check if you're on the right path for you. See if you're putting in continuous effort and if you're learning to grow.

December 31ᵗʰ

Inventory.

Another year has gone by and with it all it's good and bad experiences. To be honest it doesn't matter whether we've managed to do everything or not. It's okay, we're only human. There is also nothing to get upset about if things didn't go the way we wanted. We're walking the path of life. Sometimes there are unexpected turns and bumps along the way and that's all a part of it.

This is the time to take stock of all the qualities you were blessed with and of all the people around you: friends, family, colleagues, customers, dogs and cats. You aren't alone in life! You're lucky! If the path of life leads you downhill eventually you will begin to walk uphill again. The important thing is to continue walking and appreciate everything. Take nothing for granted.

Take a few minutes to contemplate what you have and feel grateful! You'll be pleasantly surprised.

In Judaism there's a proverb, "May it be the end of the year and its curses. A new year and its blessings shall begin."

In this proverb there is a blessing for opening a new page in the new year free from all the difficulties of the previous. This is an opportunity to give thanks to the life that has brought you this far. Every ending is a new beginning.

Remember that in the end everything is alright!

Made in the USA
Las Vegas, NV
27 June 2024

91567359R00216